ADVENTURES IN
PAPER PIECING & DESIGN

A Quilter's Guide with Design Exercises, Step-by-Step Instructions & Patterns to Get You Sewing

Sarah Elizabeth Sharp

stash BOOKS®
an imprint of C&T Publishing

Text copyright © 2018 by Sarah Elizabeth Sharp

Photography and artwork copyright © 2018 by C&T Publishing, Inc.

PUBLISHER: Amy Marson

CREATIVE DIRECTOR: Gailen Runge

ACQUISITIONS EDITOR: Roxane Cerda

MANAGING EDITOR: Liz Aneloski

EDITOR: Christine Doyle

TECHNICAL EDITOR: Julie Waldman

COVER/BOOK DESIGNER: April Mostek

PRODUCTION COORDINATOR: Tim Manibusan

ILLUSTRATORS: Tim Manibusan and April Mostek

PRODUCTION EDITOR: Jennifer Warren

PHOTO ASSISTANT: Mai Yong Vang

Collage and instructional photos on pages 2–5, 9–11, 15, 17–28, 30, 32, 37–39, 41, 51, 53, 57, 59, 65, 73, 75, 77, 89, 95, 103, and 144 by Eric Lubrick (ericlubrick.com)

Styling by Anna Marisa Martinez

Style photography by Lucy Glover and flat-shot photography by Mai Yong Vang of C&T Publishing, Inc., unless otherwise noted

Published by Stash Books, an imprint of C&T Publishing, Inc., P.O. Box 1456, Lafayette, CA 94549

Library of Congress Cataloging-in-Publication Data

Names: Sharp, Sarah Elizabeth, 1985- author.

Title: Adventures in paper piecing & design : a quilter's guide with design exercises, step-by-step instructions & patterns to get you sewing / Sarah Elizabeth Sharp.

Other titles: Adventures in paper piecing and design

Description: Lafayette, CA : Stash Books, an imprint of C&T Publishing, Inc., 2018.

Identifiers: LCCN 2017057936 | ISBN 9781617455575 (soft cover)

Subjects: LCSH: Patchwork--Patterns. | Quilting--Technique.

Classification: LCC TT835 .S4634 2018 | DDC 746.46/041--dc23

LC record available at https://lccn.loc.gov/2017057936

Printed in China

10 9 8 7 6 5

DEDICATION

For my family:

To my husband, Sam, who always wanted me to write a book … though I'm quite certain this wasn't what you had in mind.

To my three joyful, fiery, and nonpareil daughters—Jettie, Florence, and Nell—you are pure bliss.

To my siblings, for all the love.

And to my parents, for affording me the desire to fish (and for teaching me to quilt—thanks, Mom).

ACKNOWLEDGMENTS

A very special thank-you to everyone who helped with *Folksy Friends*: Nicole Buckley, Nicole Calver, Amanda Castor, Ben Darby, Erin Davis, Allison Dutton, Joshua Helms (also known as Molli Sparkles), Anneliese Johnson, Amanda Kattner, Adrianne Reid, Alison Robins, Sarah Schraw, Nicole Shipley, Anne Sullivan, Angie Wilson, and Kristy and Shayla Wolf.

My sincere thanks to my fellow plant lady, Heather Givans. Thanks also to the wonderful longarm quilters who quilted tops for the book—Rachael Dorr, Marion McClellan, Andrea Munro, Karlee Porter, Kathleen Riggins, and Angela Walters—without you, I'm just a piece-maker. I owe my gratitude to all the individuals and companies that contributed fabric and notions for the book: Alison Glass and Andover Fabrics, Inc.; my favorite local quilt shop—Crimson Tate (and the CT crew!); Daylight Company; Me+You (and Aaron, too!); Oakshott Fabrics; Paper Pieces; Robert Kaufman Fabrics; Windham Fabrics; and Quilters Dream Batting.

Finally, thank you to my amazingly understanding team at C&T Publishing. You all *rock*.

Contents

Introduction

Spoiler alert: I'm a total puzzle nerd. Not just the jigsaw kind, either—I'm talking about those mind-bending, mental-acrobatics–type exercises that leave you scratching your head but unable to think about anything else. Suffice it to say, when I first stumbled upon foundation paper piecing, the attraction was immediate. Mysterious markings on papers that magically fit together and transform fabric into super-graphic designs? Pretty much my dream come true. And the best part? *All puzzles have solutions.* You just have to understand the mechanics so you know how to stay on track (and what to do if and when you veer off course).

It just so happens I've spent years making mistakes with this method. That's where this book comes in: *Adventures in Paper Piecing & Design* is the culmination of all my trial, error, and takeaways since paper piecing my first block all those years ago. It provides the tools to thrive when confronted with just about any paper-piecing challenge, from straightforward sequences to the Mount Everest of designs. Along the way, you'll build (or reinforce) a solid skill set, learn how to break down patterns, and ultimately create designs of your own.

You'll accomplish this in three parts:

I. A detailed overview of the foundation-paper-piecing (FPP) method (the building blocks, if you will)

II. An introduction to FPP design (that is, designing your own patterns)

III. Design exercise prompts, paired with my own narrated example, to help you master the process and get your creative juices flowing

One note about the inspiration for this book: As the saying goes, it's literally everywhere. For both the prompts and my takes on them, I chose accessible subject matter (think traditional blocks, typography, and everyday items like houseplants and bugs) so that you could use this as a workbook of sorts and draw upon your own muses for any given exercise. To be sure, I've poured so much of myself into this book—from the backstories to the collage boards to the narratives behind the blocks. Still, I've tried to do it in a way that encourages *you* to explore *your* process rather than feeling confined to mine. To that end, consider this book a springboard for your own personal foundation-paper-piecing adventures.

And in that spirit … here we go!

Part I

The Method

First things first—what is foundation paper piecing? How do you sew on paper? Do you need special tools?

In this first section, I walk you through the method I've developed for all my paper-piecing escapades, covering everything you need to know to go from cryptic lines and numbers on paper to a finished fabric block.

A glimpse at what lies ahead!

What Is It?

Foundation paper piecing (FPP) is a technique that involves sewing on a foundation—in this case, paper. The patterns operate as your guide. Straight lines indicate where to sew, and numbers indicate the order in which to sew.

Sample foundation

That said, it can take a little time to get your bearings. Unlike traditional piecing, there's always a foundation (the paper) *on top* of the fabric when you position it on the stitch plate of your sewing machine. It can feel like sewing blind at first (which, admittedly, can be a little disorienting). But like most everything else, it just takes some getting used to!

... But Why?

Paper-piecing patterns are crafted so that intricate designs can be stitched in a way that maintains their precision without requiring über-exact sewing.

Though one could theoretically achieve the same results with a meticulous ¼″ seam, perfect stitch lines, and unparalleled sewing prowess, foundations help the rest of us mortals look as though we, too, have superhuman sewing powers.

The Tools

We'll drill down on the method in the next chapter, but first let's talk shop.

PAPER: Oh, the great paper debate! Some people feel very strongly about the types of paper they'll use for their foundations. I am not one of those people. I'm pretty low-maintenance when it comes to paper choice—thin printer/copy paper usually does the trick, is readily on hand at my house, and is easy on the wallet. Plus, lighter-weight paper (think filler paper or twenty-pound computer paper) facilitates fairly easy tearing yet is substantial enough to stand up to intricate designs.

Tip
HOW PAPER CHOICE AFFECTS STITCH LENGTH

Keep in mind that the thicker the paper, the shorter the stitch length should be. I'll talk about stitch length in a bit. But for now, just know that it takes more force to tear thick paper, so you'll want the perforations from your stitch lines to be closer together than you would with a lighter-weight paper. If your stitches are too far apart, you may end up ripping your stitching along with the paper.

But regular printer paper is just one option. Here are a few others:

Newsprint: Newsprint, or newsprint-thin paper made especially for FPP (think Carol Doak's Foundation Paper by C&T Publishing), is lighter than cheap copy paper. This is both a blessing and a curse, depending on the complexity of the design. Less-intricate designs involve fewer stitch lines, so newsprint holds up pretty well, with the added bonus that it tears away very easily. Detailed designs, however, require something heftier to ensure the paper stays intact from the first seam to the last (and the many in between!).

Vellum, tracing, or tissue paper: Translucent papers are a good option if you're working with limited light. Their inherent see-through nature can be a big help when positioning your fabrics. Again, thinner paper (such as tissue paper) is better suited to simpler designs.

PATTERN-TRANSFER MATERIALS: There are a few traditional ways to transfer paper-piecing patterns onto your foundation (the paper): a printer, copier, or a pen or pencil. For most designs, especially more detailed ones, I prefer to print them right onto the paper. You can also replicate them by hand (using tracing or vellum paper) if you're making a limited number of blocks. If you go this route, a lightbox or window can be very handy for this exercise.

Alternatively, for blocks you plan to make multiples of, you can quickly create "copies" of the patterns by perforating the papers with an unthreaded sewing machine needle. To do this, simply affix one copy of your pattern to the top of a small stack of plain papers trimmed to match the original pattern size. (If you don't have easy access to a printer, just trace the block so you can retain the original for your files.) Secure the stack together with a clip. Stitch through all lines in the pattern using a standard stitch length (approximately 3.0), puncturing the paper as you go. You'll be left with perforated "print" lines. You can either hand write the piecing order on each pattern copy or refer to the original as you piece. (Plus—as I'll discuss in the next chapter—those same punctures will act as a tactile guide to "see" where to place your fabric once you start piecing.)

Tip

PAPER NEEDLES?

Hang onto used sewing machine needles instead of throwing them away. They may be too dull for fabric, but they're usually fine for perforating foundation papers.

WRITING UTENSILS: One great thing about piecing on a foundation is the ability to make notes right on the pattern. Whether you prefer to jot down shorthand notes about your color scheme or color the entire pattern, steer clear of crayons. You'll be ironing the fabric after it's attached to the foundations; things can get a bit sticky if crayon wax is involved!

CUTTING TOOLS: In an ideal world, you'll have two pairs of scissors (one for fabric and one for paper), a rotary cutter, and a cutting mat. Confession: I tend to grab the same scissors for everything—my go-to gold Gingher shears. I'm sure one day dull blades will come back to bite me, but for now, one pair does the trick.

THREAD: I am a cotton purist and have historically used neutral 50-weight cotton 99 percent of the time. Occasionally, I'll swap out my go-to neutrals for a colored spool if I'm concerned about light thread being too visible against a darker fabric. If you're a polyester person, some companies have started offering finer cottonized options that boast less bulk and near-invisible seams (for example, Wonderfil's DecoBob 80-weight thread), which really do live up to their reputation and just may make me a full-on cottonized convert before long. No matter what you choose, just make sure to test them in your machine to see if they play together nicely.

NEEDLES: Select your machine needle just as you would for any other project: based on the fabric and thread you're using. I use Superior's titanium-coated topstitch 80/12 needles for just about everything, though sometimes I go a little smaller (70/10) when working with really fine materials. Try to resist the temptation to select a larger needle (90/14 and up) just to better perforate your papers. You risk damaging your fabric with the oversize holes when you can adjust your stitch length (or perhaps try out a different paper) to achieve the same result.

PINS OR GLUE STICK: Whether you're a newbie or not, using pins or a glue stick to secure the first fabric piece of each section to the pattern can be a huge help. It means one less moving part to keep in place, which is especially helpful for larger pieces of fabric.

RULER WITH ¼″ GUIDE: A ruler with a ¼″ guide is a must. Although you can eyeball seam allowances as you add areas *within* each section, you'll want a precise ¼″ seam allowance around the perimeter of your completed section patterns. This ensures accurate piecing when you go to assemble those block sections into the whole pattern and then assemble the completed blocks into your finished quilt.

Add-a-quarter rulers are pretty much designed expressly for this purpose. These rulers have a ¼″ lip, so there's no need to scan the entire ruler for the ¼″ line. It makes trimming a breeze as you're piecing. I own a couple of these rulers and have tried to integrate them into my routine, but I still find myself reaching for my two favorite quilting rulers—3½″ × 9½″ and 6½″ × 12½″—over the add-a-quarter ones when I trim my block sections. Like many things, it's a matter of personal preference, so do what makes the most sense to you.

SEAM RIPPER: Because mistakes happen! But really, this one will become self-evident as you go on.

SEAM ROLLER: This unassuming little tool is a great time-saver when piecing sections with smallish pieces. Just make sure to get one with a rounded barrel to prevent fabric distortion.

IRON: While rolling (or finger-pressing) seams is okay for small areas, I find an iron really does the best job of making sure everything is in its proper flattened place before sewing down subsequent areas, especially when dealing with big pieces of fabric. Likewise, ironing finished sections before joining them into a block helps ensure your pattern points line up as they should.

TAPE: Tape comes in handy for two reasons. First, when mistakes do happen (see Seam Ripper, page 13), overly perforated patterns can start tearing apart before the section is fully pieced. A little tape helps keep everything together without having to resew the block on another piece of paper. Second, large-scale (or enlarged) patterns that print on multiple pages must be joined before you can start sewing, and transparent tape is the perfect solution for that. Either way, it's worth having on hand.

I find matte or satin clear adhesive tape works well, but just about any single-sided tape will do. Just avoid heavy-duty tape such as packing tape. Packing tape is a tad *too* strong and makes paper more resistant to tearing. While this is a good thing if you're trying to mail an important package across the country, it's bad news if you're trying to remove paper foundations from your quilt block.

THE WACKER: This wacky, mallet-like notion helps flatten overlapping seams into submission.

Your Workspace

SEWING MACHINE: I have a no-frills, straight-stitch–only machine that I love. Your machine doesn't have to be fancy. However, I will say that the extended table for my machine is worth its weight in gold—that extra workspace is perfect for assembly-line piecing or laying out the fabric for whatever section is next in the queue.

When paper piecing, you will want to reduce your *stitch length* from the standard 2.5–3.0 down to 1.5–1.8 (or thereabouts). The reduced stitch length helps perforate the paper so that it tears away without compromising the seams you've sewn. Additionally, the stitches won't be *so* small that they shred the pattern as you sew. If your paper doesn't seem to be holding up, bump up the stitch length a notch.

LIGHT SOURCE: Sewing by sunlight is a luxury in my house, so I find it helpful to have a good light source nearby. For the longest time, I used whatever light happened to be overhead in my designated sewing space. Recently I got a lightbox, and I have to say, it's a game changer. Whether you opt for a tabletop lightbox or a simple desk lamp next to your machine is a matter of personal preference. Either option will be a huge help with fabric placement and alignment, as sufficient lighting allows you to see the fabric through the foundation.

IRONING BOARD: A mini ironing board can be a great time-saver for pressing as you go, but an ironing board, whatever the size, is a must.

Tip

SET YOURSELF UP FOR SUCCESS

Paper piecing can be a production without the right setup. To streamline the process, set up an ironing or seam-rolling station to the dominant side of your sewing machine, and keep a good light handy on the other side. I'm right-handed, so I keep a little ironing stool to my right and my light source to my left.

The Piecing Method

Now that I've covered what foundation paper piecing is and the tools you need to do it, how in the world do you foundation paper piece?

First things first: the paper-piecing patterns. My preferred method of foundation paper piecing involves whole paper patterns (page size permitting) that are cut apart and then reassembled in fabric. Before the cutting, it's a lot like a paint-by-number image, except that the notations correspond to a piecing order rather than a color guide. To start getting comfortable with the method, let's take a look at a sample pattern.

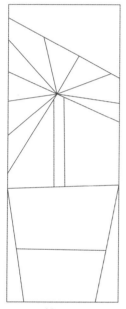

Banana Leaf foundation design

Pieced Banana Leaf block

Tip

MIRROR, MIRROR

Because the printed side of the pattern is the *back* of the finished block, the printed pattern is a *mirror image* of the finished block. So while it looks like the banana leaf is leaning left, it'll finish on the right, as pictured.

FINISHED BLOCK: 3½″ × 9″

Anatomy of a Foundation-Paper-Piecing Pattern

Patterns are made up of lines and numbers. All the lines are connected, but only some intersect, and each space has a letter or number within it (or both). So what does it all mean? When the pattern is cut into sections and sewn in the right order, each new stitch line builds upon the last, until the entire section is covered in fabric and you can't add anything else.

As you will see from the illustration (page 16), this is only possible when you *cut the pattern* along the line separating sections A and B. Put a different way, each section is a self-contained, continuous unit that must be pieced separately from the other. There is simply no way to add the A areas to the B areas, or vice versa, without some crazy inset seams. They *must* be pieced independently of one another.

OUTER SEAM: PAPER EDGE

The edge of the paper represents your exterior seamline. Remember what I said earlier about cutting things apart before sewing them back together? The sections, once pieced, turn into traditionally pieced patterns, and the cuts you made to separate them are simply the seams required to reassemble the block.

Because of this, your fabric should always extend at least ¼″ *past* the edge of the paper; this is your standard seam allowance for when you go to join the sections back together.

INNER SEAMS: INTERIOR LINES

The solid lines within the edges of the paper are your sewing lines. This will make more sense as you go, but these are the seams that can be joined in succession until everything in that section is pieced. Just as in regular piecing, you'll have ¼″ seam allowances along these lines, too, but they will be hidden between the fabric and the paper pattern.

SEQUENCE MARKERS

Each space or area within a pattern is labeled with a number in single-section patterns or a number and a letter in multi-section patterns.

AREAS

Areas are the basic building blocks of paper-piecing patterns, each one representing *a different piece of fabric* that, together, will make up your final design. The number notated within each area designates the order in which the areas must be pieced. That is, area A1 is the first piece in section A, followed by area A2, and so on.

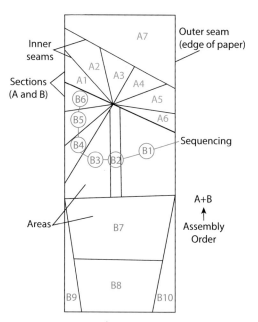

Banana Leaf pattern anatomy

SECTIONS

Some patterns are divided into smaller sections. Sections are groupings of adjacent areas that can be pieced continuously—*in a particular order*—until the entire section is covered in fabric. In my patterns, the *letter* identifies the section in a multi-section block, so all areas preceded by the letter *A* are part of section A.

ASSEMBLY ORDER

While it doesn't always appear on the pattern itself, each multi-section paper-pieced block has a designated assembly order to follow after all the individual sections have been pieced. Sometimes, as here, it's relatively straightforward: "A + B" means that once both sections are completely pieced and trimmed, section A will be joined to section B to complete the block.

Other times (take the Septopus, page 82, for instance), the assembly involves many sections that must be pieced in a more complex sequence. Again, at the assembly phase the pieced sections effectively turn into traditional patterns assembled using a standard ¼″ seam.

Foundation-Paper-Piecing Steps

Now that I've gone over the anatomy of a pattern, it's time to break down the steps to transform it from paper to fabric—banana-leaf style!

STEP ONE **PREPARE THE PATTERNS**

Transfer the pattern onto paper and cut out the individual sections as required. Once you print your copy of the banana leaf pattern (page 113), you will cut out the rectangular block and then the line dividing section A from section B.

Note: Coloring Your Pattern

If you plan to color in your pattern or make notes about which fabric to put where, do that before cutting the pattern sections apart so you can see how everything works together. Use colored pencils to turn your patterns into full-color guides, or jot down words or shorthand in each area to keep things straight. One of my go-to shortcuts is to circle all the background numbers rather than writing out "background" or "bkg" in every single area.

Tip

PAY ATTENTION TO PATTERN SCALE

Unless you *want* to change the size of the quilt block, print your pattern according to the scale provided in the pattern. It's typically 100%, but always double-check. Alternatively, you can increase (or decrease) the pattern size. Most home printers have a tile or poster print option that adjusts the scale and prints a single block across multiple pages that you (or your minions) can tape together into one big pattern before cutting into its respective sections. For really supersized blocks, trade the taped seams for a trip to the copy shop, where you can enlarge blocks into oversize black-and-white prints (also called *blueprints* or *engineering prints*) up to 36″ × 48″.

STEP TWO **CUT THE FABRIC**

Cut more than enough fabric to cover each of the numbered areas in the first lettered section. I tend to treat each numbered area (A1, A2, A3, and so on) as a template and allow for roughly ⅜″–½″ seam allowance around each piece as I cut it out. This is your *generous* seam allowance, and it should spare you some time with your seam ripper!

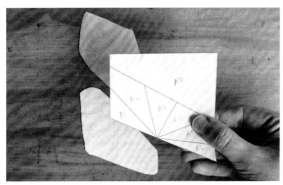

Pattern for Section A with fabric for areas 1 and 2, wrong side up

Tip

WAIT—WHAT AM I DOING AGAIN?

When paper piecing, things are turned a bit upside down and backward. One thing that helps me to keep my bearings is to remember that the printed side of the pattern is the back (and mirror image) of the finished block. When you go to cut your fabric, the wrong side of the fabric should face the wrong (unprinted or blank) side of the paper pattern.

Fabric Prep

Some folks prefer to cut each area as they're about to sew it rather than cutting out all areas for a given section up front. I'm a very visual person, so cutting everything ahead of time allows me to visualize how the colors and fabrics within the block will come together. But that's just me! If you don't already have a preference, try it both ways and do what works best for you.

Likewise, you might have already learned to paper piece using large scraps or rectangles (regardless of the area shape), with the idea that the pieces are so large they will adequately cover their respective areas even if imprecisely placed. If you've found that to be a foolproof method, by all means, carry on! However, if you are open to trying a different approach that requires a little preparation in exchange for less fabric waste and more intentional fabric placement, I encourage you to give precutting a try.

STEP THREE **PLACE FABRIC A1**

Place the fabric for A1 so the wrong side of the fabric faces the wrong side of the pattern. Hold it up to a light source to make sure it covers the whole area A1 and extends at least ¼˝ past the edges of A1 and into the bordering areas.

Only fabric within the bounds of area A1 will be visible in the finished block.

Tip

TO ALL THE FUSSY CUTTERS OUT THERE!

For placement purposes, the fabric *within* the bounds of a given area is what will show in the finished block. The portion *outside* the area perimeter is your seam allowance and will *not* be visible in the finished block.

STEP FOUR **SECURE THE FABRIC**

Once positioned, use a pin or a dab of glue to secure the first piece to the paper. Note that this step is only necessary to stabilize the *first* numbered area of any given lettered section; once areas 1 and 2 are pieced, both will be secured to the pattern by your stitch line.

For supersized areas, I sometimes use a *basting stitch*, the longest stitch length on the machine, to secure the first piece in place before adding the second. Basting stitches are easily removed after everything is assembled and tend to be more effective than pins or glue.

STEP FIVE **PLACE FABRIC A2**

After securing A1, place the fabric for area A2 wrong side of the fabric to wrong (unprinted) side of the pattern. Make sure the fabric covers the whole area and extends at least ¼˝ past the edges of A2. Note that it will—and should—overlap with A1.

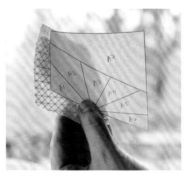

A2 fabric placed

A

B

C

D

Fold-and-Flip Method

When I flip pieces, I more or less pinch them over the sew line.

1 After lining up your fabrics so that they're right side out and adequately covering their respective areas, set the unit down on your work surface, printed side of the paper down, with the piece you are adding *closest* to you.

E

2 Holding your fabrics in place, lift up the paper just enough to fold the line separating the 2 areas you're preparing to join (the sew line separating A1 and A2). **Figs. A & B**

3 Crease that line, bringing the fabrics right sides together. You're flipping the new piece right side over onto the earlier piece(s). **Fig. C**

F

4 Leaving the fabrics right sides together *and holding them in place*, pull back *only the paper* so that once again it's flat on your work surface (printed side down). **Figs. D & E**

G

5 Unfold the first piece (A1 in this example; **Figs. F & G**). Untuck the seam allowance out from underneath the loose piece (A2; **Figs. H & I**). Your new piece should be folded onto itself by roughly ¼″—that's what you want to untuck. To prevent the fabric from shifting, use one hand to secure the main piece in place and the other to untuck the ¼″ fold.

The crease in the pattern line should line up with the crease in the fabric pieces. If the loose piece moved slightly in the flipping process, shift as necessary to realign. **Fig. J**

H

Ensure Proper Placement

After you've flipped your piece, you can check to make sure it will cover the area before you sew by simply folding the pattern back along the line you're about to sew. In other words, crease the same fold you just made, only this time with the new fabric piece positioned for sewing. If your fabric covers the entire area and then some (that is, it extends past all the area bounds by at least ¼″), you're good to sew.

I

J

STEP SIX STITCH ON THE LINE BETWEEN A1 AND A2

Taking care not to shift your fabrics, position the pattern/fabric unit on the stitch plate of your sewing machine so that the printed paper is facing up, with the fabric sandwiched between the stitch plate and the paper.

Double-check that your stitch length is appropriately reduced (page 14). Starting ¼″ out from the line, stitch along the line between areas 1 and 2, making sure to continue ¼″ after the line ends. **Figs. K & L**

STEP SEVEN DOUBLE-CHECK THE AREA COVERAGE

Open the new piece into place, right side of the fabric facing out. Finger-press the seam to ensure the new piece more than covers its area with an adequate seam allowance outside the area bounds.

If it does, fold the new piece back (right side to the earlier piece) and go to the next step. If it doesn't, get out the seam ripper and try again. (I told you that the seam ripper's purpose would become self-evident!)

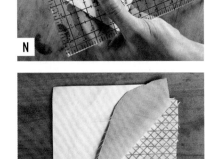

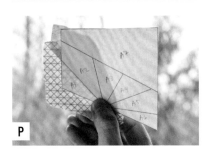

STEP EIGHT TRIM AND PRESS THE AREA SEAM ALLOWANCE

1 Fold the paper back onto itself, away from the line you just stitched. **Fig. M**

Note: Trimming Seams That Intersect Earlier Sew Lines
For new seams that intersect with previous ones, you may need to pull some of the earlier stitch lines away from the paper to be able to free the seam allowance for the area you just sewed. To do so, gently lift those earlier seams from the paper, stopping at the seamline you just sewed, and trim your seam allowance to ¼″.

2 Holding the paper away from the seam, measure ¼″ from the line you just sewed. (You can eyeball it or use a ruler to be more precise.) Trim any excess fabric. **Fig. N**

3 Unfold the paper and press the area you just added. **Figs. O & P**

Tip

HOW TO AVOID DARKER SEAMS SHOWING THROUGH

In traditional piecing, the rule is to press seams toward the darker fabric. But because seam direction is predetermined by the piecing order (seams are effectively pressed under subsequently added areas), you don't exactly have that option in paper piecing. To avoid darker seams showing through when adding an area with light fabric to an area with darker fabric, allow a little more seam allowance than normal when cutting your lighter fabric piece. Trim the seam allowances separately so that the light fabric *extends past the dark fabric* by about ⅛". When the light fabric is pressed onto itself with this extra overlap, it will help prevent the darker fabric from showing through.

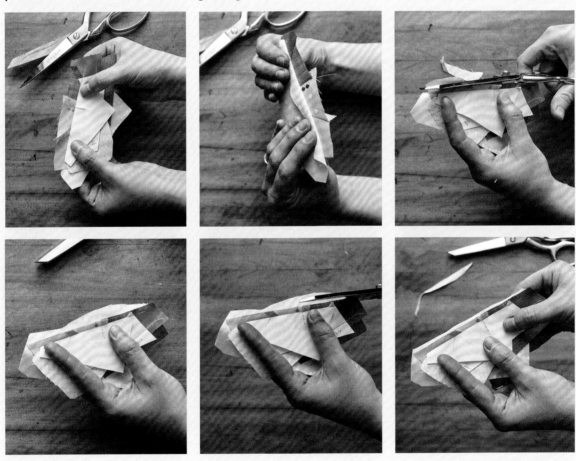

STEP NINE **REPEAT FOR ALL AREAS IN THE SECTION**

Just like you did for area 2, repeat the basic process for the remaining areas in numerical order (3, 4, and so on) until you have pieced all areas of the first lettered section. At that point, the section A pattern will be entirely covered in fabric, with at least ¼" of fabric extending past all edges of the paper.

Assembly-Line Paper Piecing

When sewing multiples of the same block, I like to streamline the process. For instance, I cut out everything at once, piece all like sections at once, trim at once, assemble at once, and so on.

First, I recommend cutting out one full block to make sure you're happy with the color distribution and confident that the pieces are the right size. Once you've done that, *use that first set of pieces as templates to cut the rest.* If you go with this method, I find it helpful to arrange the pieces in little stacks (for example, a stack of A1s next to a stack of A2s next to a stack of A3s), right sides down in the same layout as the final pattern (**Fig. Q**). Place markers noting the respective area on top of each stack to keep track of what's what. Once you've cut out all your pieces, chainstitch identical block sections required for your design (for example, all A2s to A1s, then A3s to A2s, and so on). Proceed to the next step.

Q

Little stacks for all areas in section A, laid out for assembly-line paper piecing

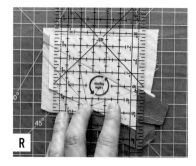

R

STEP TEN
TRIM THE SECTION SEAM ALLOWANCE

Using a ruler with a ¼″ guide, measure ¼″ from the outer edge of the paper. **Fig. R**

Trim the excess fabric beyond the seam allowance. Repeat until all edges have been trimmed. **Figs. S & T**

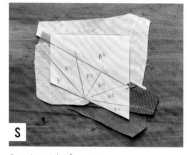

S

Section A before trimming

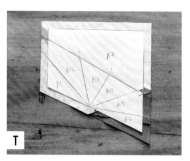

T

Section A after trimming

STEP ELEVEN
REPEAT FOR ALL SECTIONS

Repeat the process until you have pieced and trimmed all the lettered sections that you need for the block. **Figs. U & V**

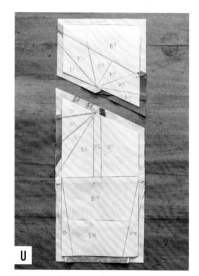

U

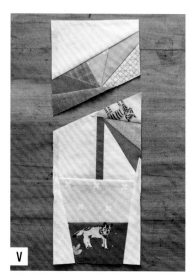

V

Sewn and trimmed sections for Banana Leaf block—back and front

STEP TWELVE **SEW THE SECTIONS TOGETHER**

Now it's time to assemble. First, reset the stitch length on your machine. (Recall that you reduced it earlier to better perforate your pattern papers.) Lengthen the stitch length to what you normally use for piecing, around 2.5.

After you've trimmed all the lettered sections of the block and before removing any papers, join block sections in the order designated by the pattern. For the Banana Leaf block, it's simply A + B. As you join the sections in their respective order, sew right *along* the edge of the paper—that is, the outer seamline you cut earlier. That's your sew line. Press as you go.

Line Up Critical Points

Use the corners of the paper to help line up the lettered sections. For instance, with sections right sides together, stick a pin into the corner of the first section and out of the corresponding corner of the second to ensure proper alignment. **Fig. W**

For more complex patterns, like some of those in *Folksy Friends* (page 78) or *Jungleview* (page 99), place pins through *all* points that should match up in the design, not just the section corners.

STEP THIRTEEN **REMOVE THE PAPERS**

Remove the papers from your assembled block. **Fig. X**

STEP FOURTEEN **REDUCE BULK IN THE SEAMS**

If you have any bulky seam joints (in this case, the center spoke of the banana leaf), iron the block and use The Wacker (or a similar tool) on a firm surface to flatten them out.

W

Use pins through corresponding points in the pattern to help line up sections when piecing the block together.

X

Start peeling!

Tip
WACKY 101

Once you've pieced a block with numerous overlapping seams, remove the papers and iron the block, taking care to get those seams nice and hot. Transfer the block to a hard surface and strike the target area several times using The Wacker tool. Voila! Say buh-bye to much of that bulk!

Tips and Tricks: Plant Lady

To get more comfortable with the FPP method, let's walk through several sample foundation-paper-pieced blocks in a design I call Plant Lady. All the blocks finish at 9˝ tall, and each one presents a different challenge to help you build your skill set and confidence level.

Bamboo Shoots (below) | Dune Grass (page 27) | Tin Can Sprig (page 30) | Electric Echinacea (page 39)

Banana Leaf (page 15) | Wheatgrass (page 26) | Shell Cactus (page 28) | Fern Rose (page 32)

Straight Lines: Bamboo Shoots

Straight lines at 90° are about as simple as it gets when it comes to foundation paper piecing. For those of you just starting out, this lucky bamboo is just for you!

First, let's take a look at the pattern. Just like Banana Leaf, this block is divided into two sections: A and B.

You'll notice the first area of section A is the middle strip (A1), with two A2s on either side, followed by two A3s, and so on, until you get to the last piece: a single A6. There are a couple different reasons for doing this.

It doesn't matter whether you start with A1, A2, A3, A4, or A5. Parallel seams separate all those areas, so you can add to either side without affecting the other. Because they don't intersect until A6, starting with one or the other changes the direction of the seams but nothing else.

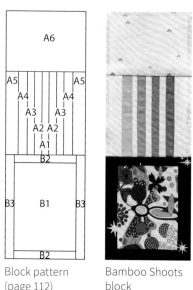

Block pattern (page 112)

Bamboo Shoots block

FINISHED BLOCK: 3˝ × 9˝

Additionally, by starting as close to the center as possible, you can then add (and press) two areas at a time instead of just one as you get farther out. It may seem like a small thing, but it helps speed up the process, especially if you're assembly-line piecing a boatload of bamboo.

1 Follow along with the steps laid out in Foundation-Paper-Piecing Steps, Step One through Step Three (pages 17 and 18). Once you have your pieces cut, place the fabric for A1 with the wrong side of the fabric to the unprinted side of the pattern, and secure it in place with a pin or a dab of glue. Choose your fabric for one of the A2s, and place it wrong side down to cover one of the 2 areas adjacent to A1. Once it's in place, flip it over the sew line and sew it in place as outlined in Step Six (page 20). **Fig. A**

Note: Placing Straight Areas

With straight lines, it's generally not necessary to use the fold-and-flip method described in Step Five (page 19). Instead, eyeball the second piece over the sew line so that the fabrics are right sides together, making sure there's at least ¼″ of fabric extending past the sew line. Because there aren't any angled joints in this block, you know ahead of time exactly where a flipped strip of fabric is going to wind up—perfectly parallel to where it is now.

2 Now that you've sewn the first A2, trim your seam allowance and finger-press that area flat and out of the way before moving on to the second A2. Repeat the sequence above to place the second A2; then press both flat with an iron. Repeat piecing both and pressing both for the next several areas, all the way up to A5. Then add A6, trim the seam allowance, press, and trim the section.

It's the same story for section B: You can piece both B2s, press, and then repeat with the B3s to finish the section. **Fig. B**

3 Trim section B; then sew the 2 sections (A + B) together into your finished block.

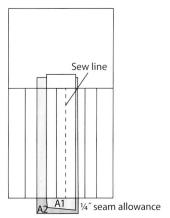

A   First bamboo shoot, flipped over the sew line and ready to sew

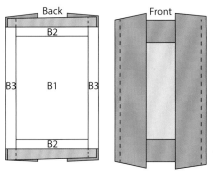

B   Section B with both B3s sewn in place and ready to be pressed and trimmed

Tip
FUSSY-CUT SPOTLIGHT

The (relatively) large, framed area in B1 provides a great opportunity for a fussy-cut pot!

Use large areas as a focal point for your favorite fabrics.

Angles: Wheatgrass

My, my, my … what sharp angles you have! But don't worry—that's what makes foundation paper piecing *look* more complicated than it actually is.

In my experience, angles trip up people the most when they try to eyeball the flip over the sew line. When you eyeball the flip, you inevitably lay the new piece slightly skewed from the sew line. And when you sew that seam, one of two things happens: you end up with an inadequate seam allowance (that is, less than ¼˝ on one or more sides) or the new piece doesn't quite cover its intended area.

To take out some of the guesswork, I highly recommend the fold-and-flip method described in Step Five (page 19).

1 After you've placed and secured the fabric for B1, position the fabric for area B2 so that it adequately covers and extends past the area boundary by ¼˝ on all sides. **Fig. A**

2 Using the fold-and-flip method described in Step Five, fold your pattern at the seamline, making sure to crease both the paper *and* the fabric sandwiched between it. Because you just made sure the B2 fabric covered all of area B2, you can be fairly confident that the line you just creased in that fabric is the right seamline to join it to the preceding pieces.

3 Follow the rest of Step Five (page 19). Before advancing to Step Six (sewing B2 in place), carefully check to see that the creases line up as they should before sewing them together. If they do, sew B2 in place, press it, and get ready for the next piece!

Admittedly, *extreme* angles present their own challenges. My solution? After much trial and error, I've found it best to simply cut a *really* generous (½˝–¾˝) seam allowance around highly angled points (here, all the wheatgrass and background areas in section A). It may be a little more wasteful, but it pays off in time and the frustration saved.

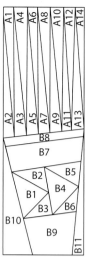

Block pattern (page 112)   Wheatgrass block

FINISHED BLOCK: 3˝ × 9˝

Back   Front

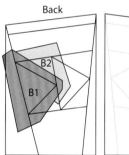
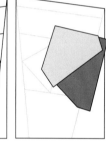

A Adding area B2

Directional Prints: Dune Grass

Using directional prints in paper piecing is really just a matter of a little planning, some patience, and fussy cutting. To illustrate this point, let's use only directional fabric in this Dune Grass block.

1 MARK PATTERNS: First, make some notes on the pattern pieces. **Fig. B**

GRASS: For the grass in section A, I want the stripes in the fabric to follow the sway of the grass, so I've drawn lines in my desired direction in each grass area.

POT: To keep things interesting, let's place half of our striped fabric horizontally rather than following the existing diagonal lines for all the pot areas in section B.

2 USE THE PATTERN NOTATIONS TO ALIGN THE PRINT: When you come upon an annotated area, use your notes as a guide to properly orient the print when you're positioning the fabric right side out—that is, *before* the flip.

For instance, when you place the dune grass fabric to ensure the fabric adequately covers a particular area, double-check that the stripe orientation is running in the direction your notes say it should be. If not, take a step back and think about what needs to be changed. Reposition or recut your piece as needed. **Fig. C**

3 PIECE THE REMAINING AREAS: Continue to assemble the block in this manner until everything is pieced.

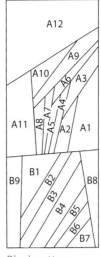

Block pattern (page 113)   Dune Grass block

FINISHED BLOCK: 3½″ × 9″

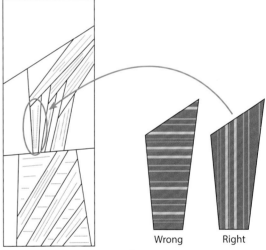

B Mark up the patterns (your cheat sheet for directional prints).

C Pay attention to directional fabrics!

Wrong   Right

Tip

PLACING SUBSEQUENT AREAS

When adding directional prints to a section that already contains part of that print, the already-pieced area is arguably an even more helpful guide than your notations on the back. When you place the new piece to ensure it adequately covers the new area, any overlap with the old area should visually blend together. And this makes sense because the idea is that the print flows seamlessly between the various areas. So any time a new area overlaps an old one during placement, everything should absolutely align.

Tiny Piecing: Shell Cactus

Small scraps are perfect for tiny piecing, right? *Not so fast!* A perfect fit isn't always a good thing when you're piecing on a small scale. In fact, the trickiest part about tiny piecing really isn't tricky at all—just make sure you cut your fabric pieces with a more generous seam allowance than normal. (This can feel a bit unnatural when the seam allowances are bigger than the area you're trying to cover!)

Let's take area 6 for example. Cut a piece to cover area 6, and make it at least 50% larger than you ordinarily would. It sounds so simple—and that's because it is! Instead of fumbling around with a piece the size of a pinky nail, you will have a little wiggle room when you go to add background area 6 to the main plant, all thanks to that additional seam allowance. It seems like a small thing, but just a few fractions of an inch will make it easier to maneuver those areas when you place and flip them for sewing.

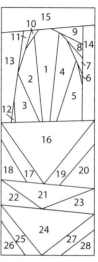

Block pattern
(page 114)

Shell Cactus block

FINISHED BLOCK: 3½˝ × 9˝

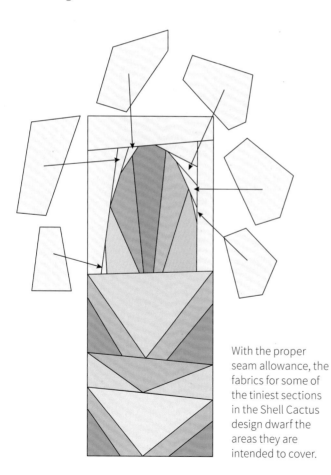

With the proper seam allowance, the fabrics for some of the tiniest sections in the Shell Cactus design dwarf the areas they are intended to cover.

Tip

MAKE IT COUNT

Given the relatively small size of your fabric when tiny piecing, you'll want to make it count. Be sure to use fabric with high contrast to get the biggest impact from that teeny, tiny space!

Keep an eye on the contrast and relative value of small pieces to make the most of those tiny slivers of fabric. Note that the lower contrast on the right (medium blues next to medium greens) loses some of the impact achieved by the higher contrast coloring on the left (medium greens next to low-volume creams and whites).

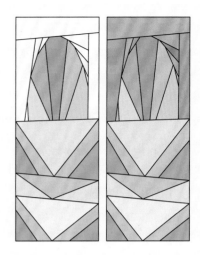

PIECING SEQUENCING

Do you notice any areas that can be pieced in a different order? Take a closer look at the Shell Cactus block.

- The first area can be 1, 2, 3, 4, or 5. **Fig. A**

- Area 12 can be pieced at any time after area 3.

- Area 10 can be pieced after areas 1 and 2. **Fig. B**

- Area 14 can be pieced at any time after area 9. **Fig. C**

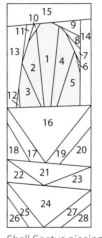
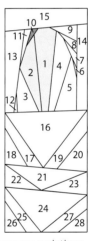
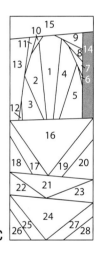

Shell Cactus piecing sequence variations

Tip

WHAT ABOUT THE LITTLE GUYS?

Okay, you caught me! *Technically* area 12 (or even area 6) could also be the first piece. However, it's much more cumbersome to add a large area to a tiny one than to add a tiny area to a larger one when it comes to the first piece. Because of this, always make the larger of the two areas the first, unless you have a really good reason not to (for example, you want an *über*-exact fussy-cut print in the smaller area, or you have concerns about a darker seam showing through). If you do make the tiny area the first, use a dab of glue or a small pin to secure it in place before positioning the larger area 2.

Curved Piecing: Tin Can Sprig

Curved paper piecing is really just piecing curves after sewing paper-pieced sections that happen to have curved edges. As you may have already guessed, unless you've got some crazy magic tricks up your sleeve, it really isn't possible to paper piece with any accuracy or effectiveness along a curved line. Instead, those curved lines are necessarily *block* or *section boundaries*. In other words, after assembling all the lettered sections, some will finish with curved edges. So you'll just have to sew a curve to assemble rather than straight piecing as you would along a straight line.

CRASH COURSE IN CURVED PIECING

1 TRIM THE CURVED SEAM ALLOWANCE TO ¼″: As you'll recall, my FPP patterns do not include a ¼″ paper perimeter (the seam allowance), which means you will have to trim fabric seam allowances beyond each paper section after piecing. Curved sections are no different.

When trimming curved seams, use a quilting ruler with a ¼″ guide and line up the ¼″ mark (usually a dashed line) with the paper edge at one end of the curve. Slowly move the ¼″ guide along the paper curve; think of the paper edge as a track for the ¼″ line. Mark the seamline with a contrasting fabric pen until the length of the seam is marked, or just trim as you go using scissors or a small rotary cutter. **Fig. A**

2 MAKE YOUR MARKS: The patterns themselves have little registration-type marks that straddle the curved lines (**Fig. B**). (You can also add some of your own before cutting apart the sections.) When you go to reassemble the curved sections, you can stick pins through the matching points to ensure they'll line up the same way you would use pins to line up straight section edges.

I also like to mark my fabric ¼″ in from either end of a given section. Because you have paper patterns, this will simply be the point (or imperfect "corner") of the paper.

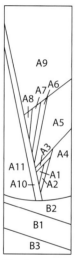

Block pattern (page 115)

Tin Can Sprig block

FINISHED BLOCK: 2½″ × 9″

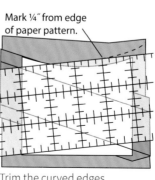

Mark ¼″ from edge of paper pattern.

A Trim the curved edges of the block.

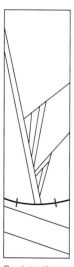

B Registration marks on pattern

3 ALIGN YOUR CURVED PIECES:

PIN METHOD: Line up the 2 sections you're joining, right sides together, and place a pin through any or all of the registration marks you made in Step 2 (previous page). *Remove the paper from the inner/concave curve.* Slowly sew the pieces together, removing pins as you go. Then skip ahead to Step 6.

SINGLE-PIN METHOD: I usually don't have the patience for pins, especially for small sewing like this. To sew curved pieces with just one pin, place the outer/convex curve (the plant) on the inner/concave curve (the pot), right sides together. Line up the edges where you will start to sew by sticking a pin through the end point of the paper where the curves meet (¼″ in from the fabric edges).

Note: Dog-Ears

When you join two pieces at any sort of angle, the ends don't match up evenly the way they do with straight piecing. Instead there will be a dog-ear of overlap, with the seamlines syncing up about ¼″ in from each end.

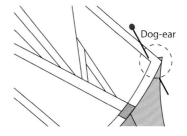

4 REMOVE THE PAPER FROM THE INNER CURVE: For the single-pin method, sometimes it's helpful to remove some or all of the paper from the inner/concave curve before sewing. This allows for a little more give in that section as you join the pieces together. Remove the paper after you've placed the pin that is aligning the 2 sections. The downside of removing the paper is that you will lose registration marks, which you might need later if things don't line up quite right.

5 JOIN THE INNER AND OUTER CURVES: Once the first end is aligned, remove the pin and slowly sew the pieces together with the outer curve (the sprig) on top, shifting the edges into alignment as you go. **Fig. C**

6 SNIP OR NOTCH THE SEAM ALLOWANCE: Whether you use the pin or single-pin approach, you may need to clip or notch the seam allowance to release some of the tension so the joined unit lies flat. Whether you snip or notch depends upon the direction you press the seam, which is typically influenced by the fabric color. I always try to press toward the darker fabric where possible. If pressing the curved seam toward the inner curve (the pot), cut triangular notches out of the seam allowance, like a jester's collar. If pressing toward the outer curve (the sprig), cut small snips into the seam allowance just up to the stitch line, like fringe.

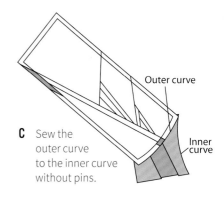

C Sew the outer curve to the inner curve without pins.

TROUBLESHOOTING THE SINGLE-PIN METHOD

If things aren't coming together as they should, try tacking down both ends of the curve and then working toward the middle. Using the ¼″ marks as your guide, line up the first set of ends with right sides together. Backstitch that point in place. Check the alignment by flipping the two pieces open to make sure that end point aligns when the sections are right side out. Repeat the process with the other end; then sew the rest of the curve together. This way you know from the start that the ends will line up, and everything in between should even out. And if all else fails, just pin everything together from the start!

Freezer Paper Piecing: Fern Rose

One of the first things you'll notice about the Fern Rose is that it can be pieced continuously in a single section. Use that to your advantage to learn an alternative to traditional foundation paper piecing: *freezer* foundation paper piecing. The two main differences between standard FPP and freezer FPP are that you will print your pattern onto freezer paper and that you won't sew through the freezer paper. Because of this, you can use each pattern multiple times, which makes it an attractive option for single-section (and otherwise uncomplicated) designs.

1 PRINT THE PATTERN ON FREEZER PAPER: The easiest way to prepare your pattern is to use a printer-ready sheet of freezer paper to transfer the FPP pattern onto freezer paper. Alternatively, you can trace the pattern lines onto the *matte* (non-shiny) side of the freezer paper. Once you've transferred the pattern, cut out the pattern along the section lines to remove any excess paper.

2 PLACE THE FABRIC: Place the fabric that covers area 1 just as you would if you were using the standard FPP method. Once it adequately covers the area, iron it in place. Take care to place the iron only on the fabric—*not* on the freezer paper, which will stick to the hot iron. **Fig. A**

Block pattern
(page 114)

Fern Rose block

FINISHED BLOCK: 3″ × 9″

Again, just as you would with FPP, place the second piece of fabric to ensure it adequately covers area 2 before flipping it over the sew line. **Fig. B**

Flip area 2 over the sew line so the pieces are right sides together and ready to be joined. **Fig. C**

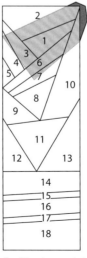

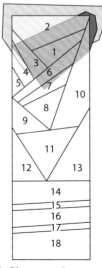

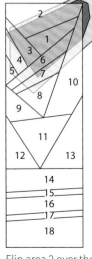

A Positioning area 1

B Place area 2.

C Flip area 2 over the sew line.

3 FOLD BACK THE PATTERN ALONG THE SEW LINE: *Before sewing the pieces together*, fold the freezer paper pattern back onto itself along the line separating areas 1 and 2. Ordinarily, you would fold back the paper *after* sewing areas 1 and 2 to your foundation. Here, you fold it back *before* sewing them together and use the paper edge as a guide for your stitch line, just as you do when joining 2 FPP sections together. **Fig. D**

4 STITCH ALONG THE FOLDED PAPER EDGE: Making sure to keep everything in place, stitch right along the *edge* of the folded freezer paper. **Fig. E**

5 TRIM THE SEAM ALLOWANCE TO ¼″: Keeping the freezer paper folded back, trim the seam allowance to ¼″ (**Fig. F**). Press the area 2 fabric so that both pieces are right side out. Continue piecing in this manner until the entire section is assembled.

6 TRIM THE SECTION SEAM ALLOWANCE: Once you finish piecing the whole section, trim the section, leaving ¼″ of fabric extending past the paper edges.

7 REMOVE THE PAPER: Peel off the freezer paper and reuse for another rose!

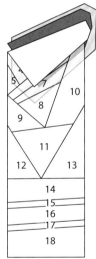

D Fold freezer paper back along line between areas 1 and 2.

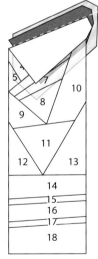

E Sew area 2 to area 1 along folded edge.

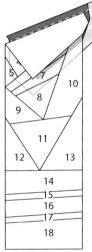

F Trim seam allowance to ¼″.

Plant Lady Quilt Assembly

Materials

BACKGROUND: 6 yards of assorted low-volume solid fabrics

MAIN: 3 yards of assorted light to dark blue, turquoise and green fabrics

BACKING: 3½ yards

BINDING: ⅝ yard

BATTING: 58″ × 78″

1 I mentioned earlier that all the blocks in the Plant Lady design finish at 9″ tall. (See the _Plant Lady_ patterns, pages 112–115.) To piece your plants into a finished quilt, lay out the blocks in rows of your desired width. Add 9½″-tall background strips of varying widths between the blocks to achieve your desired layout.

2 Separate the rows with thin strips between each row to create a plant showcase of sorts. For the sample, I kept the shelving simple with unpieced strips, but feel free to get creative! Use a combination of thick and thin horizontal strips to add dimension or use rows of continuous Flying Geese pieced end to end for an even fancier display. Whatever you decide, I recommend using an overall height of 1½″–2½″ for the shelves.

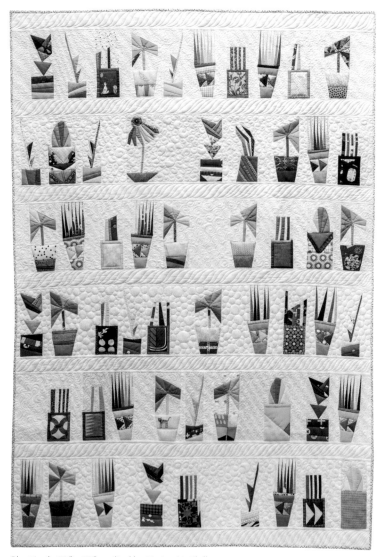

Plant Lady, 50″ × 70″, quilted by Marion McClellan

3 Sew the rows of plants together. Join the rows to the alternating rows of shelving strips.

4 Trim, assemble your backing, sandwich, and quilt as desired.

HOUSEWARMING PLANTS

Nothing says, "Welcome home!" quite like a stitched plant that doubles as an essential oil warmer. Whether you're sending housewarming wishes to an old friend or welcoming a new neighbor, the potted Plant Lady blocks are the perfect mouthpiece for that message. Personalize the pots using text fabrics (can you spot the hidden "hello"?), or ad-lib the designs to express something more effusive.

1 After you've pieced your plant and removed the papers, cut a piece of backing the same size as the unfinished plant block.

2 Place the plant block and backing right sides together.

3 Sew *almost* all the way around the perimeter, leaving a 2″ opening to turn the warmer shell right side out.

4 Turn the warmer right side out.

5 Fill it about three-quarters full with your filling of choice. I like flaxseed—it is said to have optimal heat-retention qualities—mixed with a few drops of essential oils and some dried lavender.

6 Stitch the opening closed.

7 Heat it in the microwave for a minute or so, and enjoy. . . .

8 . . . for a moment. Then break out some ribbon and gift that plant lest you get too attached!

Part II

Design

The first time you design a paper-piecing pattern you may feel that it's a little bit like putting together a puzzle. Except all the pieces are blank, you're blindfolded, and someone may or may not have just spun you around a few times. Sounds fun, right? But fear not! This section is meant to do away with that blindfold and teach you how to fill in all those blanks.

GETTING STARTED IN
Foundation-Paper-Piecing Design

Inspiration

Inspiration is literally everywhere: nature, photographs, artwork (be mindful of copyright!), wildlife, and even elements that aren't obviously visual—think sayings and song lyrics. With very few exceptions, I find this to be true: If you can get it on paper, you can probably paper piece it.

Tools

THE BASICS

Just as with the piecing method itself, there are some basic tools you will need for the design process. As you can tell, it's nothing too fancy.

Pencils // Sketchbook paper // Ruler // Eraser // Tracing paper

Another helpful tool? A lightbox. It's totally not required but handy nonetheless.

ADVANCED TOOLS

If you have access to and are comfortable using computer design software like Adobe Creative Suite, great! Though I use Photoshop to finish most of my pattern designs these days, more often than not I start the process with good old pencil and paper. In this book, I'm going to approach pattern design the old-fashioned way, but feel free to improvise on the computer if it feels more natural to you.

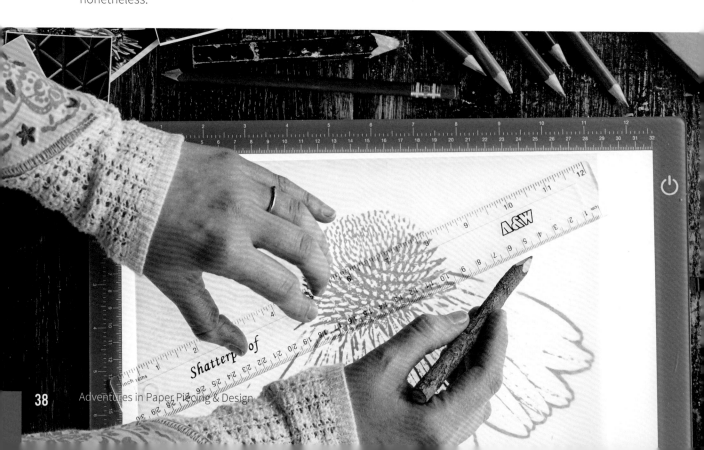

Adventures in Paper Piecing & Design

The Design Process

How to Approach Pattern Design

By this point, you've had an opportunity to see a number of different patterns and how they're constructed, and that's a good thing—spending time with existing patterns is a great way to get more fluent in the language, so to speak. But you likely picked up this book because you're more interested in learning how to design *your own* patterns rather than studying someone else's. Let's use the Electric Echinacea block to do just that!

Tip

For a refresher on commonly encountered shapes and how to break them down, check out: www.nohatsinthehouse.com/adventures.

Although I drafted all but one Plant Lady block freehand, inspiration always comes from somewhere. For me, of late, it's Justina Blakeney's "jungalow" style, which features eclectically decorated spaces where electric green plants abound. So while I didn't have any one particular image of a banana leaf in mind (or on paper) when I sketched my Banana Leaf block, there were no doubt countless snapshots of that plant imprinted in the back of my mind when I drafted it.

Electric Echinacea block

FINISHED BLOCK: 4½″ × 9″

But because you can't read my mind, and because I don't always draw everything ahead of time these days, I designed one of the blocks using a stock photo of a coneflower to help illustrate my every step (and misstep).

Photo by iStock.com/BubblegirlPhoto

Echinacea stock photograph

Tip

COPYRIGHT

In the U.S., images and artwork are subject to copyright. This isn't my area, so I'm not an expert by any means. However, if you plan to sell your patterns, enter them into shows, or do something else that goes beyond your own personal use, you'll need permission from the copyright owner (for example, the artist or photographer) if you choose to use their work as a starting point for your own. I purchased the rights to the stock photo at left for the purposes of this book.

STEP ONE **CHOOSE YOUR INSPIRATION**

If you are new to pattern design (or working on complex patterns), it's helpful to start from something concrete rather than trying to reconstruct an idea freehand from memory. Whether you start with a photograph or have your eye on something around the house (such as flowerpots), be sure to have a reference image handy when you sit down to design the FPP pattern.

Tip

GETTING IT ON PAPER

When your inspiration isn't already captured in a photo or a drawing, the exercise of translating that initial inspiration from the intangible into something more concrete is an important step in the pattern-design process—especially when you're just getting started. Sketching freely without worrying about section lines or sequencing order ensures you'll be pleased with the overall look, feel, and composition of your eventual pattern. In fact, I consider it to be an essential step in the design process. Otherwise, it can be a little daunting to dive straight into pattern design from a fuzzy image in your head.

STEP TWO **PREPARE THE REFERENCE SUBJECT**

Use a photocopier to enlarge your reference image or sketch to a workable size. This does not have to be the absolute final size—you can always scan it and scale it later on. For now, you just want to be working with something more substantial than a thumbnail.

When I design, I tend to scale up images so they're at least letter size. If you're using computer design software, just scan the image and resize it directly in the program.

Create an Outline Version of Your Reference Subject

After adjusting the image size, overlay a piece of tracing paper on the reference photo. Make sure you can see your reference subject well enough to make out the details you want in your design. If not, create an *outline* version to serve as your reference for drafting your pattern. You can distill your subject to an outline by hand or use an online tool (search the internet for "create outline of image") or app (Sketch Me! or FX Photo Studio have a handy pencil outline effect).

A low-contrast reference image may not show clearly through tracing paper.

An outline of the image may be easier to work with.

Now comes the fun part! Using *only* straight lines for now, break down the image into a workable pattern outline. Remember, straight lines = sewing lines!

Tip
WHY NOT CURVES?

It's not possible to piece along a curved line *within* a foundation section, which is why I suggest you limit yourself to straight lines for the time being. However, as discussed in Curved Piecing: Tin Can Sprig (page 30), curved lines in paper-piecing patterns are totally on limits—but they have to be *section edges*.

1 *Get Out Your Tracing Paper*

Lightly tape your image to your work surface, and place a sheet of tracing paper on top of it. Tape along the top of the tracing paper to ensure your papers don't shift as you're working. This will also allow you to flip between the tracing paper and the inspiration image.

2 *Identify Your Block Bounds*

Consider whether you want your reference subject centered in your background, partially cut off, or something else. I wanted the flower more centered in my finished design, so I've drawn a rectangle to frame it accordingly. Anything on the reference subject that's outside of the rectangle will not be part of the finished design. **Fig. A**

A Electric Echinacea block outline marked on inspiration image

Tip
THE RULES

It's natural to wonder whether there's a set of hard-and-fast rules for pattern design. *What's the maximum number of adjoining seams? How many sections is too many? Just how small is too small?* Frankly, it's fairly subjective, so the most informative limits to the design process will be *your own*—not anyone else's. What's too much or too tiny for one person may be entirely tolerable for another. Rather than approaching pattern design as a black-and-white process with clear dos and don'ts, spend some time in the gray (and at your sewing machine) to understand how different design choices translate into fabric—and how you feel about that.

3 Mark the Main Sections

When breaking down the pattern, go from general to specific. Rather than heading straight for the nitty-gritty flower bud details, start with the main divides in the pattern—in this case, simply separating the object from the background space. To achieve this, use a pencil to draw straight lines that extend all the way to the block edges, along the line where the flower meets the background (**Fig. B**). If your reference subject is not divided into a well-defined foreground and background, look for other logical divisions or prominent elements to use as a starting point.

Don't worry about setting anything in stone now—that's what the eraser is for! Just start drawing the lines that feel natural to you. If they don't look right, erase and try something else.

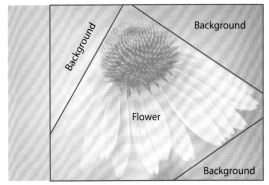

B These three lines separate the foreground (the flower) from the background.

Tip
PRELIMINARY PIECING ORDER

As you draw, it's good to keep piecing order in the back of your mind. At this point, you can tell from looking at the drawing that the flower area will necessarily be further broken down and thus pieced first, with the background sections added last (in no particular order, since none of them overlap one other).

4 Mark the Areas (The Details!)

Now that you've identified the outer bounds of the flower, start giving it some dimension. To do this, subdivide the area with straight lines that follow the contours of the flower. In this case, there are two predominant features—the spiked bud and the petals. Mark a line between the two, and then take each in turn. **Fig. C**

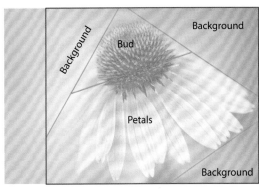

C Main foreground sections (petals and bud)

Tip
DEPARTING FROM THE REFERENCE SUBJECT

Very few subjects are suitable for (and worthy of) a 100 percent literal conversion into an FPP design. That would involve infinitely more sections than are generally necessary to document every last detail. In this photo, the bud really cuts into the petals in a U-shape, which would result in one of three things if you wanted to precisely re-create the image: a curve, a Y-seam, or several small sections that chop up some of the petals. As I mentioned earlier, we're designing without curves for now. So unless you want to sew a Y-seam when you go to reassemble your pattern sections, use only straight lines that extend edge to edge (or line to line) to mark the pattern areas. To avoid unnecessarily small sections, ask yourself if you can still preserve the spirit of the image without capturing every last detail. If the answer is yes, then chop off that bud!

MARK THE AREAS OF THE BUD

Paper-piecing patterns can be as detailed as you and your sewing machine will tolerate. Here, I wanted this flower head to finish at 3½″ wide or less (like the other Plant Lady blocks), so I made the conscious choice to let some of those delectable spikes go. If I were designing a 30″ pattern, there would be spikes as far as the eye could see!

After you've considered the design details you're willing to let go, start by breaking down the contours you want to *keep*. Remember, just because you're working in a small space doesn't mean all those beautiful features should fade into a shapeless blob. Rather than preserving every last spike, include a select few in your drawing. Once the echinacea bud has a little personality, give the rest of it some shape with a few more lines until you can make out the bud. **Fig. D**

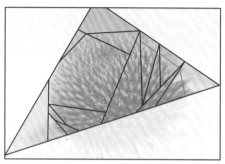

D   Bud attempt 1

There are a couple things to note here. First, the creative liberties! (A big spike in the middle? Sure, why not?) Second, note the short lines (**Fig. D**, in orange) between the spikes that define the bud. Although this accurately captures the bud's full rounded shape (otherwise, it would just be jagged spikes), it does so in a way that creates multiple section lines when it doesn't necessarily have to—so let's turn to that.

Assess the Piecing Order of the Bud

We'll revisit this in Step Four: Finalize the Sections and Sequencing (page 47) but as I mentioned earlier, I'm always thinking through piecing order as I go. I want to walk through that now within the bud section. First, let's identify the areas that have to be pieced first.

How do I find the first piece, you wonder? That's a good question! Remember *T H*! The best way I can describe it is to search the sketch for the capital *T*'s (perpendicular or slanted intersecting lines) and *H*'s (more common in sections with near-90° angles, like the petals, next page). Why, you ask? Well, the two adjacent areas *below* the top line of the *T* must be pieced before the area *on top* of the *T* can be joined to them. So anytime you see what looks like areas below a *T*, you know they must *precede* the area above the *T* in the piecing order.

Can you spot all the *T*'s?

Likewise, the areas between the two outer lines of the *H* must be pieced before the areas on its side can be joined (assuming they can be at all—where *H*'s or *T*'s butt up to one another, it is likely that the top of the *T* or the sides of the *H* will be *section* lines). That's what is happening with bud attempt 1. **Fig. E**

Note the *adjacent* (or intersecting) *T*'s. For example, A1/A2 and B1/B2 share the line between sections A and B. It's the same story with the C's, D's, and E's, where those short lines along the outer bud create intersecting seams (that is, C1/C2, D1/D2, and E1/E2). Recall that areas under the *T* (or in between the parallel lines of the *H*) must be pieced first. Because of this, the bud—as drafted—has five areas that must be pieced first, and the whole unit can be pieced in no fewer than five sections. However, I make it a personal goal to piece in as few sections as possible—so let's try this again. **Fig. F**

Notice how the outer bud is now defined by lines that extend all the way to the bud section bounds that we started out with (**Fig. F**, in orange) rather than the newly created spike lines. By making that small drafting adjustment, we have gone from five sections to just one. This is closer, but now I'm not sure I'm happy with the overall shape of the bud. It feels a little lopsided. Back to the drawing board! **Fig. G**

By changing a few seamlines, you can start with the center of the bud and continue building upon it until the entire bud section is pieced without needing to split it up into multiple sections. Pencil in the tentative sequencing on your paper. (Remember, you can tweak your design at any time—even as you're sewing the block.)

MARK THE AREAS OF THE PETALS

Moving on to the petals, you're going to have to make similar decisions about just how much you want to honor the original inspiration. Due to the target finished size, I'm comfortable losing some of the space between the petals where they come out of the bud. I'm also okay with more square-shaped petals, and fewer of them, at this relatively small scale. **Fig. H**

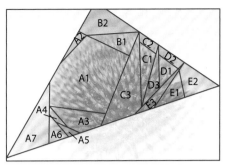

E   Bud attempt 1 piecing order

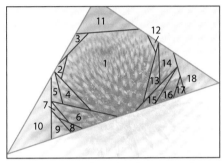

F   Bud attempt 2 with updated piecing order

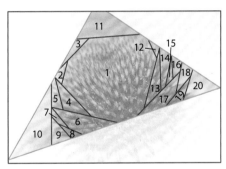

G   Bud attempt 3 with updated piecing order

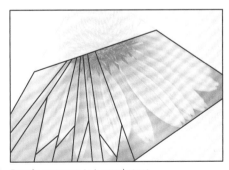

H   Petals attempt 1: A good start

Note how we are defining the petals: first by extending lines from the bud section boundary at the top *all the way down* to the next intersecting line, and *then* adding definition with shorter lines at the ends of the petals (**Fig. I**, in orange). If we only penciled in partial lines, we could wind up with inadvertent Y-seams. (Eek!)

Here I've honed in on just a few details (the V shape of the petal ends) to add interest with more straight lines. However, those short lines that define the ends of the petals (generally drawn between two new lines versus from an existing line to a new line) probably mean multiple sections. Let's take a look.

Assess the Piecing Order of the Petals

Just as you did with the bud, identify the first piece(s) in the pattern. Again, it looks like I have several starting points for several different petal sections. **Fig. J**

Note the multiple *H*'s (A1/A2, B1/B2, C1/C2, D1/D2, and G1/G2) and *T*'s (E1/E2 and F1/F2). Now that I've seen how the petal shapes play out with the piecing order, I'm going to be more mindful of my intended starting point. Though I could start in the center and work my way to each edge, I want the petals to look a little less symmetrical, so I'm going to consciously draw the next set of lines working from left to right. As I'm drawing, I'm trying to make sure the lines always intersect at least one existing line (that is, one of the four lines we drew to mark the background, bud, and petals). It may seem counterintuitive, but by starting in this manner (on the left), the first piece will be one of the last areas I draw (on the right). Once again, pencil in the piecing order based on the exercise you just did.

Figs. K & L

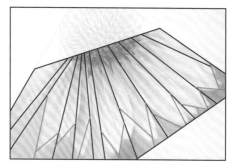

I   Petals attempt 1 with more details

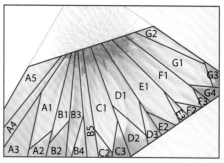

J   Petals attempt 1 piecing order

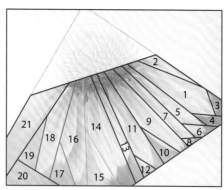

K   Petals attempt 2: Looking better—but this time, I forgot about the stem!

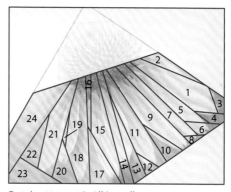

L   Petals attempt 3: All is well.

STEP FOUR FINALIZE THE SECTIONS AND SEQUENCING

Now that most of your lines are penciled in, let's think about how all these lines will translate into a sequenced paper pattern. No matter how much experience you have, you'll almost always need to redraw certain lines to extend them or change the overlap—and thus the piecing order. That's just part of the puzzle!

You already had a little preview of this with the bud and petal sections (pages 44–46), but it's time to make some final calls.

1 *Mark the Sections*

Now that you're nearing the end of the pattern design process, let's *mirror the block* before you pencil in your final piecing sequence (that is, flip it along the vertical).

When you first got started, the flower was one big section with three background sections. Now you have two flower sections—the bud and the petals. A and B will be your first two sections because you can't add either of the upper background sections without first joining the bud to the petals (your *H*, if you will—though it more closely resembles an *A*). **Fig. M**

Looking at the freestanding background sections together with the background areas in the flower sections, there's no reason that the lower left background section can't be part of section B. (It can be pieced anytime after B13.) Let's update the markings! **Fig. N**

The two remaining background pieces are unpieced sections (that is, standard patterns that aren't sewn to the fabric like paper-pieced sections). If this block were larger, I wouldn't think twice about leaving these be. However, my personal preference is to avoid loose background pieces in a 3½″-wide block. To remedy that, I'm going to extend the line separating flower sections A and B so it crosses both upper background areas. The background areas above the line can be pieced as a part of section A, and the ones below become part of section B. **Fig. O**

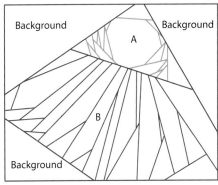

M Mirrored Electric Echinacea block with section and area markings

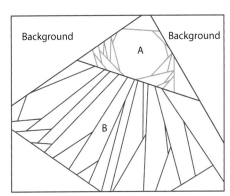

N Electric Echinacea block diagram with lower background piece now part of section B

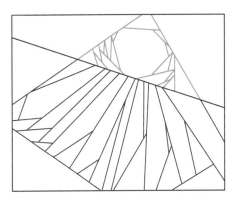

O Electric Echinacea block with upper background areas split between sections A and B

2 Mark the First Piece of the First Section

Let's turn to the two block sections and clean up any stray lines as you finalize the patterns. First, you need to mark which piece to place first (area 1) in the bud section (we're going to use A). This is largely predetermined by the sequencing exercise in Step Three (page 44), but now is the time for any last-minute changes.

Tip
REMEMBER TO LOOK FOR THE *T* (OR *H*)!

As you get more and more familiar with paper-piecing patterns, things will start to jump out at you. Within no time you'll be seeing capital *T*'s and *H*'s every time you look at a pattern. Remember that trick to single out the first area in a given section. If you think about it, it makes perfect sense: You have to piece areas that are parallel to one another before you can piece anything they intersect (like the top of the *T* or the sides of an *H*).

3 Number the Adjoining Areas Until You Hit an Imperfect or Intersecting Seam

Next, you have to see what piece(s) can be added to area 1 without overlapping the areas you haven't yet numbered. If you did your homework, this should get you all the way through the section. However, since you just made a change to the section lines, you have some residual dividing lines to clean up. **Fig. P**

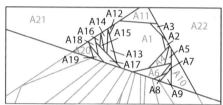

P Because the bud is section A, all the numbers are preceded by an A. Note the two new background areas A21 and A22. At this point, I've numbered as many sequential areas as I can in the bud.

Note: Sequence markers should always be placed *within* the area they define, if at all possible. Given the microscopic nature of this particular pattern, my fine editors reasonably concluded that leader lines would be a more suitable alternative to size 4 font—you have them to thank for keeping legibility top of mind!

4 Assess Whether You Can Design Around the Intersecting Seam

Once you hit intersecting seams (here, the flower petals), determine if you can piece the design in a different way. In this case, that would mean the petals would have to somehow cover the entire bottom half of the bud pieces, which would change the orientation of the petals from semi-vertical to horizontal. That just doesn't jibe with our echinacea goals.

So if the answer is no, as it is here, bold the edges of the section (for example, the perimeter of section A) to finalize those markings. Otherwise, try to rework the line placement to draw your way out of unnecessary sections!

5 Repeat the Process in the Remaining Sections

Use the same approach to figure out how to sequence the petal section. Again, most of the work should be done at this point, but now is the time to rework the background into as few areas as possible. **Fig. Q**

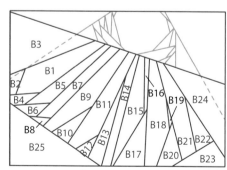

Q Because the petals are in section B, all the numbers are preceded by a *B*. Note that the previously freestanding background section is now B25, although it could be any area after B13.

TEST THE BLOCK

Or in my case, send the pattern to your friend Heather. After graciously attempting to sew the block, she sent me this text:

> *The Echinacea block is cool but holy moly.*
> *I started it but aborted mission.*
> *I'll try it again but enlarge. ENLARGE. XOXOX.*

And in that spirit, the 3½″-wide block grew into a 4½″-wide block, with a few other minor tweaks—including the addition of the stem and a simple saucer pot.

This is a section line because the areas above and below it cannot be pieced continuously (that is, there is no way to sew the A areas and the B areas on a single paper pattern). Sections must be cut apart before they can be pieced.

First area of section B can be B1, B2, or B4. Just as with section A, I chose B1 because it is the largest of the four.

B23 can be pieced at any point after B13.

First area of section C can be C1, C2, or C3.

First area of section A can be A1, A2, A5, or A7. With few exceptions, the *largest* potential first area should be area 1. Why, you ask? When it comes to piecing, it's generally less cumbersome to secure a smaller second piece to a larger first piece, rather than the other way around.

Note that areas B14–B21 extend from one section edge (the line between A and B, or B and C, or the pattern edge), and the boundary of a subsequent area. For instance, the line between B17 and B18 extends to the boundary of B19. This enables those areas to be pieced continuously.

C7 can be pieced after C5.

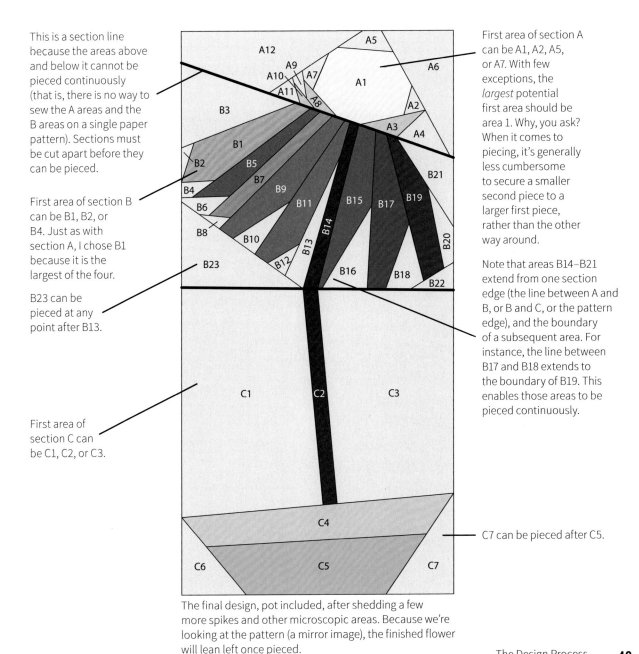

The final design, pot included, after shedding a few more spikes and other microscopic areas. Because we're looking at the pattern (a mirror image), the finished flower will lean left once pieced.

The Design Process **49**

MY APPROACH TO
Fabric, Color, and Design

If the color-order nature of this book hasn't yet given it away, I have a thing for analogous color schemes. That tendency to take the long way around the color wheel often plays out in my designs. But that ring of color isn't my only guide in the design process!

Fabric Selection

Whether you're pulling fabric from the shelves of your own stash or your local quilt shop—or some combination of the two—you've got to narrow down the universe of infinite color combinations somehow. Amy Butler once said, and I'm paraphrasing here, that no two people see color in exactly the same way. That rings true for me, and I wholeheartedly believe you should embrace that unique perspective—because if not you, then who? Color is subjective and personal, and I really encourage you to explore what combinations intrigue and attract your eye. For me, it's almost always neutrals plus an analogous set of colors. That's just my aesthetic; it's color in a way that makes sense to me.

Which analogous colors, however, tends to be guided by a design's end function. Am I creating something using a specific fabric collection, where the initial universe is necessarily limited to a couple dozen options? Is it a quilt for someone who happens to love electric green and teal? (That would be me!) Or is it for a room with a fairly well-established palette? On the flip side, maybe I'm starting with a totally blank canvas. If it's the latter, I like to turn to my favorite color-palette resources.

DESIGN SEEDS

Design Seeds (design-seeds.com) is a color blog that boasts countless premade palettes inspired by photographs from across the globe. Plus, it's got a very user-friendly interface: Search by color, season, or collection to find stored palettes to kick-start your next fabric pull.

PALETTE BUILDER

My brilliant friend Anne is the mastermind behind Palette Builder (play-crafts.com/blog/palettebuilder2/), a gadget that lets you build a totally personalized palette by pulling colors from your own uploaded images. As an added bonus, Anne's program outputs the names of coordinating solids (Kona Cotton solids and Moda's Bella Solids as of the date of this writing) and Aurifil threads, too.

Tip
FABRIC TYPE

I generally love all cottons equally and use a variety of substrates throughout my work; however, some fabrics are better suited to certain designs than others. For instance, lighter-weight fabrics (poplins, lawns, and some shot cottons) can help reduce bulk in complex designs with numerous small pieces and overlapping seams.

How It All Comes Together

My fabric-placement process is a lot like painting—except my palette is an old library reading table, which happens to be in our dining room (love you, hon). Once I have some sort of direction (for example, a palette or decor-driven color story), I'll gather whatever fabrics I want to use and start organizing them. This is where our dining room table comes in handy. Generally, I prefer to organize my fabrics by color and then value.

I'm a very visual person, so I like to physically lay (scatter?) my fabric out near whatever I'm sewing, typically in color/value order. This allows me to visualize which fabrics might go in which areas of a given block or design. Some stitchers arguably accomplish the same thing by coloring patterns ahead of time. For whatever reason, I prefer to work directly with the fabric before deciding what colors to put where.

After laying all my fabrics out, I'll start cutting. If I'm working on a design with lots of the same blocks, I'll typically cut the fabric for several blocks at once so I can piece them in an assembly line as described in Part I: The Method (page 8). On the other hand, if I'm working with an oversize block, such as the Septopus (page 132) at 400%, I'll typically cut all the background at once. Then I'll cut foreground fabric for as many sections as I can fit on my table and start piecing to clear off some space before cutting fabric for the remaining foreground areas.

(page 8), (page 132)

Tip
VALUE?

Value is the relative lightness or darkness of a given color. For an easy way to check the range of values within your selected fabrics, take a picture of your pull and apply a black-and-white filter to the image. The more variety of grays in the photo, the wider the range of values in the pull.

Tip
BE A LITTLE UNPREDICTABLE

When I piece quilts, I don't follow gradation to the letter. That is, I don't put everything in perfect color order or perfect value order. Instead, I'll arrange fabrics along a gradient, then switch a few neighboring cuts. Why bother? It pays off to be unpredictable—mixing it up gives the eye somewhere unexpected to go!

Note: Maximalism

I suppose now is a good time to note that I'm a bit of a maximalist. I often use dozens upon dozens of fabrics in a single quilt. Because I like to sew with many different fabrics, I generally use just a small amount of each one. As a result, I tend to stash pretty small cuts (think fat quarters, fat eighths, and fat sixteenths)—unless I'm totally smitten with a design, in which case I'll buy yardage and tell myself I'll use it as a quilt back one day.

Whenever I do pull a piece of fabric one yard or larger, I'll trim off whatever I think I might use for the project, taking care to include any potentially fussy-cuttable parts of the repeat. Then I put the rest back on the shelf. That way, it's more workable as I'm snipping small pieces here and there, and I don't have to wrestle with unfolding a whole yard every time I want to use an inch.

GRAFFITI
Foundation Paper Piecing

Anyone who knows me has come to accept I'm a bit of a pattern junkie. From blue banana-leaf wallpaper to patchwork Moroccan cement tiles to ocelot wallpaper paired with Aztec and plaid—it's safe to say there's no shortage of pattern in my life.

So when it comes to quilting, there's nothing I love more than a good pattern. And I'm not talking about the actual pattern (though I'm all for good design there, too). I mean the *patterning*—all the details within larger areas of a given block.

One of my favorite things to do with paper-piecing patterns is to ad-lib different graphic elements within the larger design. I'm calling it graffiti foundation paper piecing. (Thanks for the inspiration, Karlee!)

Embrace Your Inner Artistic Randomness

A friend once told me she liked my "artistic randomness." If I'm honest, my designs *are* totally random—like my handwriting, it's my personal style of whatever comes to mind. But we all have our own personal style. This is where graffiti foundation paper piecing comes in.

Note: Learn to Ignore the Lines

I struggle with publishing quilt patterns. Sometimes, they just seem so … rigid. Yes, you can re-create something to the tee, **exactly** *as I've made it.* **Or** *you can add your own artistic randomness and take the design to a place I never could. Perhaps this is a strange thing for a pattern designer to say, but what's even more flattering than someone wanting to make my design in the first place (which is admittedly hard to top) is someone who takes my design and changes it to his or her liking. In my mind, nothing tops that!*

Draft Your *Main* Pattern

If you're anything like me, you'll want to add a million little details to every pattern from the get-go. Before you do that, first try to establish the silhouette of whatever you're designing with as few sections as possible. See the forest for the trees, if you will. Focusing literally on the bigger picture will result in a better pattern, because you will be working within the natural and necessary divisions of a given design instead of patterning unfinished areas that may not jibe with the most natural divisions in a given subject.

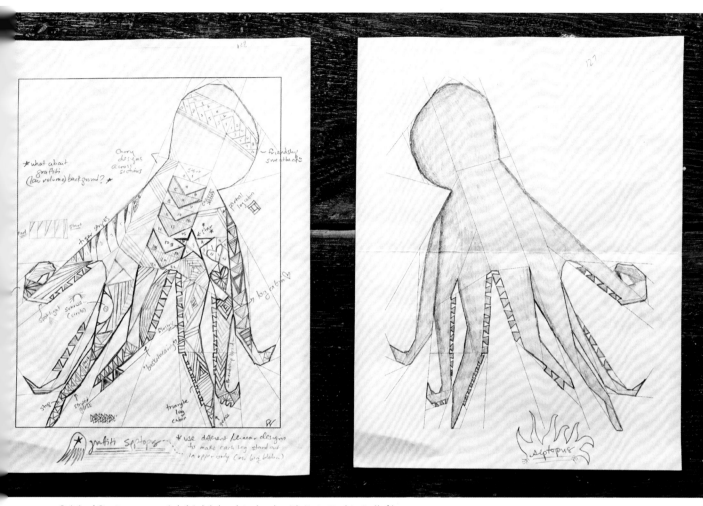

Original Septopus, pre-ink (*right*), back to back with its tatted twin (*left*)

THE OCTOPUS GAME

My husband had a pretty tight-knit family growing up. When he was younger, he made up a game called *Octopus* for his little cousins. From what I gather, he would yell "Octopus!", extend his arms out like Michael Phelps mid-butterfly, and flop on top of them. In other words, he'd smother his unsuspecting little cousins with his dead weight—*and apparently they loved it*. Having heard this story enough, I naturally wanted to stitch up a quilt featuring an oversize octopus to smother our kids with the same kind of love. Serendipitously, the Septopus block (page 132) provides the perfect canvas. I thought I'd share my thought process and my sketch to show how I'm going to approach adding graffiti FPP to the big, open spaces of the Septopus design, which I plan to enlarge by at least 500% when I turn that sketch into a reality.

Design Elements of Graffiti Foundation Paper Piecing

Some graffiti sequences can be drawn in the *first area* without requiring additional section breaks. (See What About the Little Guys?, page 29, and The Design Process, Step Five: Test the Block, page 49.) Others (like the Multi-Section Shapes, next page) necessarily create new section lines, so be mindful when placing those. You will likely have to redraw lines in neighboring sections if the area to which you're adding shapes is right in the middle of several smaller ones.

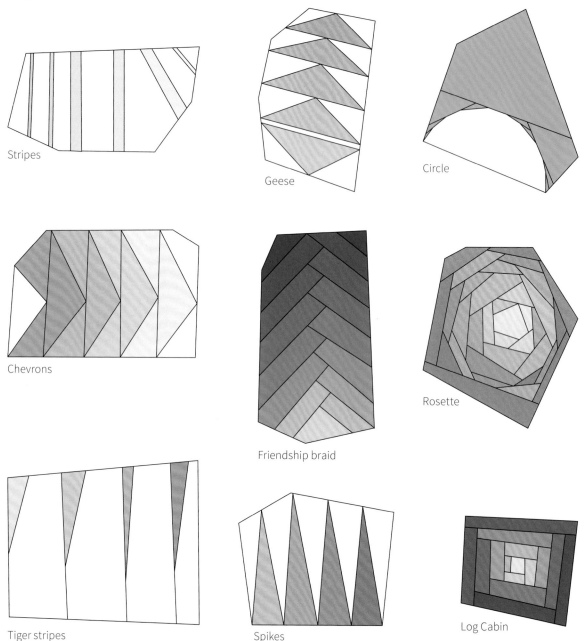

Stripes

Geese

Circle

Chevrons

Friendship braid

Rosette

Tiger stripes

Spikes

Log Cabin

THE SEESAW METHOD TO ROUNDED OBJECTS

Round subjects made up of only straight lines are totally doable without curved piecing. Which begs the question: How? I've got a method I call the *seesaw approach*.

1 First, draw a line that just barely touches one point of the circle. It should resemble a seesaw balancing on top of the object. **Fig. A**

2 Draw another line a little farther out from the first point, and extend it down toward an edge. Think of the seesaw slowly dipping down on one side. **Fig. B**

3 Add another line that extends down from the previous one. Continue to add lines in this manner, at gradually steeper angles, until a round shape emerges. **Fig. C**

4 Jot down your piecing sequence. **Fig. D**

5 Clean up any small or distracting background sections by redrawing lines across areas to hide unseemly seams. While the new area on the left helps make the background lines less distracting on that half, this now looks imbalanced (**Fig. E**). If you decide to draw a new area to cover busy seams, be sure to do it consistently to achieve balance in your design.

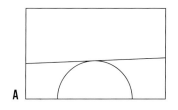

A

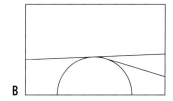

B

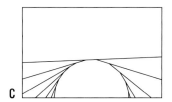

C

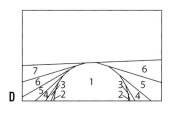

D

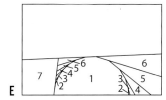

E

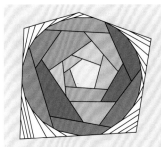

It's time to experiment! Often you can use combinations of design elements (previous page). Start with a circle, draw a rosette within it, and finish off with a few skinny stripes.

Multi-Section Shapes

The following elements require multiple sections. If you're adding elements to an existing design, identify natural breaks in the block sections where you can draw the shape across sections without creating new ones. For example, look for triangular areas that form where sections meet and use that as a starting point for the star.

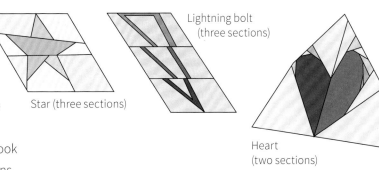

Star (three sections)

Lightning bolt
(three sections)

Heart
(two sections)

Part III

Design Prompts

This final section is workbook-style, divided into seven prompt/project pairings. Each chapter starts off with an open-ended design exercise (Design Prompt), complete with a themed inspirational collage to help get your creative juices flowing. Then I walk you through a sample project (My Take) that I came up with based on that prompt. You can use the prompt as a launching pad to create something totally new, or you can follow along with my take until you're comfortable enough with the process to go off script and create a design of your own using the techniques in Part II: Design (page 36).

P.S. If you're hoping to design your own patterns from these prompts, consider Parts I and II your required reading!

Learning by the Letter

Simple text provides a great opportunity to get your feet wet in pattern design without getting swept away. In this exercise, we'll focus on piecing methodology as you learn to separate the foreground from the background and add patterning within the bounds of a letter (see Graffiti Foundation Paper Piecing, page 52).

1 Design Prompt One

Create a Custom Sans Serif Foundation-Paper-Piecing Letter

Pick a letter—any letter—in a typeface that you find pleasing to the eye.

Tip
FONTS AND LETTERS

Sans serif letters with straight lines (think *I*, *T*, or *V* in Helvetica font) will inevitably involve fewer sections and be easier to tackle than serif or script letters with curves (*P* or *S* in Times New Roman font).

STEP ONE
CREATE AN OUTLINE OF YOUR LETTER

Either hand draw or use a word processing program to create a large outline of your letter. If you opt for the latter, size it up so the letter takes up most of the page (300- to 500-point type), format the font to create just the outline, and print.

STEP TWO
DRAFT YOUR PATTERN

Divide the Letter into Its Main Sections

Using what you learned in Part II: Design (page 36), separate the letter from the background and look for the natural dividing lines in the letter. Remember, each section consists of straight seams that build upon preceding ones. Using your ruler, pencil in the main section divides.

Subdivide the Sections

Working within one area of the letter, divide it into smaller areas that shape the letter. Keep it simple for a bold, modern look, or further subdivide those sections to create a more fanciful, patterned typeface.

STEP THREE
CREATE YOUR PATTERN

Once you're happy with the design, make a *mirror copy* of your block, scaling as necessary to your desired final size. Unless you've chosen a symmetrical letter (*A*, *H*, *I*, *M*, *O*, *T*, *U*, *V*, *W*, *X*, or *Y*) your letter will be backwards. Use that copy to create your master pattern.

Letter and number the pattern using the method in The Design Process, Step Four: Finalize the Sections and Sequencing (page 47).

MY TAKE // **SNOOZE**

Suffice it to say, I'm not exactly a morning person. If I see a clock before sunrise, all those roman numerals might as well be Z's. And that's exactly how this design came to be.

I used the font Bebas Neue for the Z's.

Snooze, 50″ × 70″, quilted by Karlee Porter

Materials

BACKGROUND

  3 yards of off-white or low-volume fabric

PAPER-PIECED SECTIONS

  <u>Clockface background:</u> 1 yard of white or low-volume fabric

  <u>Main:</u> 1 yard of assorted blues and violets

BACKING: 3¼ yards

BINDING: ⅝ yard

BATTING: 58″ × 78″

PATTERNS (pages 116–118)

Cutting

CLOCKFACE: Cut 12 from the B (wedge) pattern.

PAPER-PIECED SECTIONS: Cut fabric to cover all numbered areas from your background and main fabrics. Repeat until you have enough to make 12 Z's. **Figs. A & B**

BINDING: Cut 7 strips 2½″ × width of fabric.

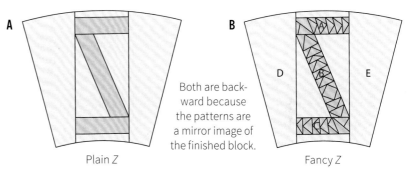

Plain *Z*

Both are backward because the patterns are a mirror image of the finished block.

Fancy *Z*

Note: Why Two <u>Z</u>'s?

The patterns (pages 116–118) include both a simple Z and an intricate Z. I chose to make one fancy Z; the rest just skip over the patterning inside the Z and can be pieced as one unit instead of cut into sections. You can do the same, or you can ignore the lines entirely and come up with your own Z for each wedge!

Clock Assembly

Seam allowances are ¼″ unless otherwise noted.

MAKE THE WEDGES

1 Paper piece the Z block. For the fancy *Z*, assemble in the following sequence (**Fig. C**):

  A + B + C // ABC + D + E

2 Sew each *Z* to a wedge (B pattern). See Curved Piecing: Tin Can Sprig (page 30). Press. Make 12. **Fig. D**

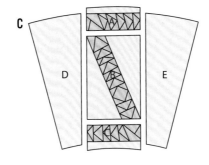

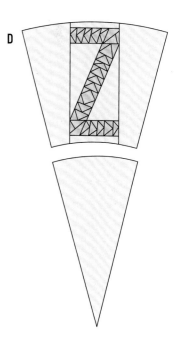

ASSEMBLE THE CLOCKFACE

1 Sew the wedges into 4 groups of 3 wedges each, making 4 quarter-circle units.

2 Sew 2 quarters together into 1 half-circle. Repeat to make 2 halves.

3 Sew the 2 halves into a circle. The circle should measure 36½″ in diameter but will finish in the quilt at 36″. **Fig. E**

Quilt Construction

1 Piece or trim the background yardage to your finished quilt size of choice. Press.

I used a 2-yard cut of 54″-wide fabric, so it required only a slight trim to yield my 50″ × 70″ desired top size. However, you can piece that same-size top using 42″-wide fabric. Just cut 2 strips 9″ × width of fabric from a 2½-yard cut of nondirectional background fabric. Sew the ends together and press. Join the long 9″ strip to the remaining 2-yard piece of background. Press, trim to 50″ × 70″, and presto!

2 Fold the top in half vertically and then again horizontally. Press the folds to mark the centerlines.

3 Unfold the top and lay it flat on a firm surface (think a wood floor or dining room table). Using a pencil, string, and fabric-safe marker, mark a circle with a 17¾″ radius (35½″ diameter) from the center of the background. **Fig. F**

4 Check your measurements; then carefully cut out the circle.

5 Because the clockface is circular, you can adjust the orientation so the *Z*'s lay exactly where you want them. (For instance, maybe you want a fancy *Z* at 12 o'clock or all the *Z*'s at the half-hour instead of the hour.) To do this, lay the clockface on top of the background, right sides up and covering the circular cutout, and rotate it until you're pleased with the orientation of the clock.

6 Once you're set on the layout, fold the clockface into quarters (in half and then in half again) to mark lines at the points where they intersect with the creases you already made in the background.

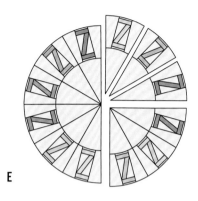

E

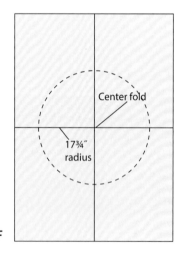

Center fold

17¾″ radius

F

7 Unfold the clockface and set it right side up on the background, also right side up. Match the 4 creases you made in the clockface with the 4 creases in the background until you're happy with its placement. Along the edge of the clock, pin the right side of the background to the right side of the clockface at those 4 points. To do this, you'll sort of fold the background toward the center of the clock as you pin right sides together. Add additional pins as necessary along the circumference to even things out. When you're done, all the background fabric will be gathered toward the center of the clockface, leaving you with a disc-shaped wad of fabric that has pins all along the perimeter. **Fig. G**

8 Using a standard stitch length, sew the background to the clockface: Sew around the circumference of the clock with a ¼″ seam allowance, removing pins as you make your way around the circle. Press toward the background.

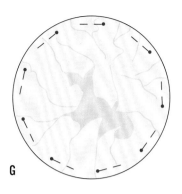

G

Finishing

Piece the backing. Layer the backing, batting, and quilt top; quilt; and bind as desired.

Traditional with a Twist

Let's face it. Sometimes the idea of starting from scratch can be a little intimidating. Traditional blocks provide an opportunity to explore elements of paper-piecing design within the safety net of time-tested patterns.

Full disclosure: I have a total weak spot for lesser-known traditional designs. There's something so alluring about patterns that have stood the test of time and have been re-created for generations, only to have faded into history books. Barbara Brackman's *Encyclopedia of Pieced Quilt Patterns* accompanies me and my family every summer when we drive to the house where my dad grew up. Each time we go, my copy gets a few more tabs and a little more worn. And with each freshly discovered block comes an opportunity to make something old become new again.

2 Design Prompt Two

Choose a Traditional Block and Change One or More Elements to Feature Foundation Paper Piecing

Whether you're drawn to simple shapes such as half-square triangles or classic pieced blocks, there's always room to put your stamp on it. Remember that the block you choose is just one part of the process. Also think about how you might use the FPP method to bring something unexpected and fresh and how those changes can enhance the overall design.

STEP ONE
TRACE THE BLOCK

Begin by tracing the block (at least 8″ × 8″, if not to scale). Make at least 2 copies for your desired finished block size. You will use the copies to test your concept; if you're anything like me, you'll need more than a couple!

STEP TWO
PLAN YOUR NEXT MOVE

Think about how you might modify the block. What sections could you change? What can you draft to complement existing elements? (Turn Drunkard's Path's quarter-circles into wheel spokes, for instance.) What can you add that is absent from the present design? (Lines? Letters? Stars? Something more abstract?) If you're having trouble getting started, it can help to preview the block in repeat so that once you start sketching (in the next step), you have an idea of how tweaks to one small area may echo and interact across the quilt as a whole.

Note: Working Within an Established Section

In the last chapter, I covered how to divide a design into main sections using letter outlines as a guide. Here, those sections are already established as the existing block outline.

Blocks of Specific Construction (2991–3012)

MAKE YOUR MARK(S)!

Working within one section of the block, divide it into new areas using the knowledge you've gained so far about pattern sequencing. Remember to keep final block construction in the back of your mind. For instance, dividing a piece with curved edges into two or more sections can make accurate sizing and trimming a little trickier than just keeping that curved piece as one section. (No matter how precise you are, seams between sections tend to add a little bulk, which in turn will change the shape of the curved piece.) If you're designing within an odd shape or a tight space, consider how you might design around potential complications.

STEP FOUR
TEST THE REPEAT

If you're planning to set your block in a traditional grid layout, test the repeat to make sure there are no surprises.

Tip
EMBRACE CHANGE!

You may choose to shift gears after seeing the repeat, but that's okay! Don't worry about getting it right on the first try. Keep experimenting, and you'll continue to learn from the experience.

STEP FIVE
CREATE YOUR PATTERN

Once you're happy with the design, make a *mirror copy* of your block, scaling as necessary to your desired final size. Use that copy to create your master pattern. Remember to add a ¼″ seam allowance to the non-FPP patterns in your new design. For the FPP pattern, letter and number the pattern using the method in The Design Process, Step Four: Finalize the Sections and Sequencing (page 47).

MY TAKE // **PRICKLY PATH**

Prickly Path, 66″ × 87″, quilted by Angela Walters

It was on one of my family's annual treks out east that I discovered Grandma's Fan—a block that, although unassuming at first glance, turns into something spectacular when repeated on point (and, evidently, with the addition of some spikes!).

To give Grandma's Fan a bit of an edge, I knew which sections to change (I wanted to add spikey triangles to the three areas that make up the outer curve lines), but I wasn't sure how to handle the repeat. The way in which the traditional block was drawn means that the overall pattern is not seamless—in other words, one of the three inner curved lines is noticeably thicker than the others, so it juts out past the two thinner lines on repeat. I could have redrawn the block and thinned out the chunky line to solve this problem, but that wasn't the exercise! Instead, I wound up drafting three potential variations on my initial spikey concept. Seeing the first two in the full layout helped me identify small changes to incorporate into the final design.

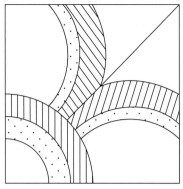

Grandma's Fan

Note how the spiky lines in the blocks help the mismatched lines to blend in. And if you're wondering *which* mismatched lines I'm talking about … well that just proves the point, now doesn't it!

Materials

BACKGROUND: 8 yards of white or low-volume fabric

MAIN: 3 yards of assorted light to dark violet, hot pink, and magenta fabrics

BACKING: 5½ yards

BINDING: ¾ yard

BATTING: 74″ × 95″

PATTERNS (pages 119–124)

Cutting

BACKGROUND: Cut 24 from each of the A, D, D mirrored, E, and E mirrored patterns.

MAIN: Cut 24 from each of the B, F, and F mirrored patterns.

BACKGROUND AND MAIN PAPER-PIECED SECTIONS: The C, G, and H patterns are the paper-pieced elements of this design. Cut enough fabric to cover all the numbered areas from your main and background fabrics. Repeat until you have enough pieces to make 24 of each.

BINDING: Cut 9 strips 2½″ × width of fabric.

FINISHED BLOCK: 15″ × 15″

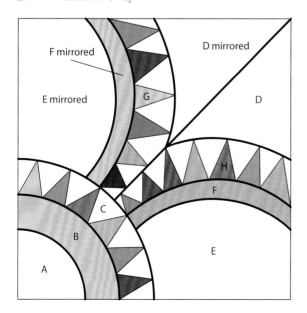

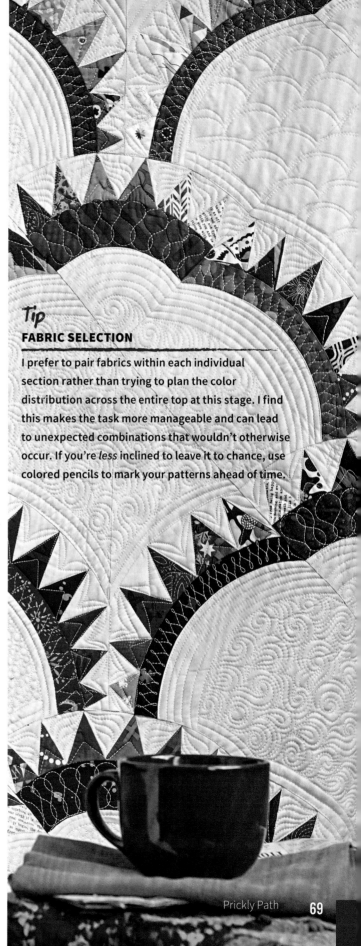

Tip
FABRIC SELECTION

I prefer to pair fabrics within each individual section rather than trying to plan the color distribution across the entire top at this stage. I find this makes the task more manageable and can lead to unexpected combinations that wouldn't otherwise occur. If you're *less* inclined to leave it to chance, use colored pencils to mark your patterns ahead of time.

Block Assembly

Seam allowances are ¼″ unless otherwise noted.

1 Paper piece the spiky sections (C, G, and H).

2 Piece and press the following block sections (**Figs. A–C**):

A + B + C (*inner curved section*) **Figs. A & B**

E + F + H + D (*half of outer curved section*) **Fig. C**

E mirrored + F mirrored + G + D mirrored (*mirrored half of outer curved section*)

3 Sew the 2 outer-curve halves together (EFHD + E mirrored, F mirrored, G, and D mirrored). **Fig. D**

4 Sew ABC (inner curve) to the combined outer curve. **Fig. E**

5 Press. Trim to 15½″. Make 24.

Note: Scrappy Fabric Placement

To achieve a scrappier look like the sample, pair a variety of pinks and purples within each block rather than repeating prints in adjacent sections.

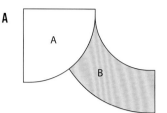

A

B

Sew the inner curve (A) to the chunky outer curve (B).

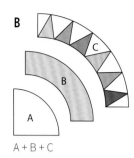

B

C

B

A

A + B + C

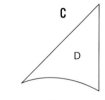

C

D

H

F

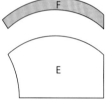

E

E + F + H + D

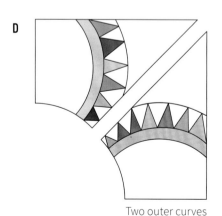

D

Two outer curves

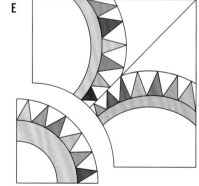

E

Sew ABC to combined outer curve.

Quilt Construction

1 Lay out 18 of the blocks on point, placing 3 blocks across on the top row and 4 blocks down. **Fig. F**

2 Of the remaining 6 blocks, halve 3 blocks vertically between D and D mirrored. **Fig. G**

3 Halve 2 blocks horizontally from the corner of E to E mirrored. **Fig. H**

4 Quarter the last block, cutting both vertically and horizontally. **Fig. I**

5 Use the 3 *left* halves to fill in the *rightmost* column of the quilt. Use the 3 *right* halves to fill in the *leftmost* column of the quilt. Use the 2 *top* halves to fill in the *bottom* row of the quilt. Use the 2 *bottom* halves to fill in the *top* row of the quilt. Use the quarters to fill in the 4 corners of the quilt top. **Fig. J**

6 Piece the blocks into diagonal rows.

7 Starting in one corner, piece the diagonal rows together to create the top. **Fig. K**

F

G
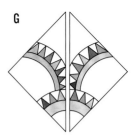

H
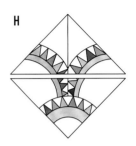

I
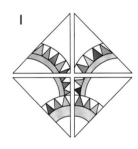

J

K

Finishing

Piece the backing. Layer the backing, batting, and quilt top; quilt; and bind as desired.

Objects

Up to this point, the section boundaries have been set for you; now it's time to try drafting those yourself. Unless you're channeling your inner Picasso, some subject matters are more forgiving than others. For instance, inanimate objects that have a wider range of acceptable shapes (feathers and bowls, for example) are slightly easier to design than, say, animals that have more recognizable features. (A short-maned lion or a stump-necked giraffe might come across as a bit odd if done unintentionally, right?) So let's start with objects where proportion is less critical.

3 Design Prompt Three

Pick an Object, Any Object!

Just make sure it doesn't move. Or have a heartbeat. Having trouble getting started? If you're in a slump, check out an online design challenge generator like ArtPrompts (artprompts.org) and click "Refresh" until inspiration strikes! Serendipitously, ArtPrompts divides prompts into several categories, including objects and creatures—it's fate! The latter may come in handy for the next prompt.

STEP ONE
DRAFT YOUR REFERENCE SUBJECT

Create a freehand design from memory until you're pleased with the composition, or choose a reference photo as your starting point.

STEP TWO
DRAFT YOUR PATTERN

Take out your tracing paper. Add, erase, and redraw the pattern lines using the method in Part II. Because you've chosen a forgiving subject, take some design liberties here! Rather than try to capture every last detail of your inspiration, try your hand at ad-libbing parts of your design or departing from your reference subject altogether. (Let's save capturing every last detail for the next exercise.)

STEP THREE
CREATE YOUR PATTERN

Once you're happy with the design, make a *mirror copy* of your block, scaling as necessary to your desired final size. Use that copy to create your master pattern. Letter and number the final pattern using the method in The Design Process, Step Four: Finalize the Sections and Sequencing (page 47).

MY TAKE // **VOODOO FEATHER PINCUSHION**

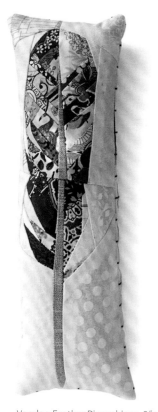

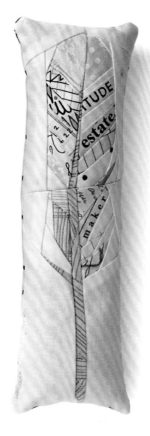

It should come as a surprise to no one that feathers have made their way into this book. Whether they're painted, dip dyed, or hanging in a dream catcher—I'm a fan. So take this Voodoo Feather Pincushion as a peace offering of sorts from yours truly. And whenever you find yourself starting to lose patience with the process, put a pin in it and think of me. (See what I did there?)

Voodoo Feather Pincushions, 9″ × 3″

Materials

BACKGROUND: 1 fat quarter of fabric

MAIN: Assorted low-volume fabric scraps

BACKING: 1 fat eighth of fabric

PINCUSHION FILLING of your choice

NEEDLE AND COORDINATING THREAD for hand sewing

PINS (naturally!)

PATTERNS (page 130)

Cutting

BACKING: Cut a piece of backing the same size as the (unfinished) feather block: 9½″ × 3½″.

BACKGROUND AND MAIN PAPER-PIECED SECTIONS: Cut enough fabric to cover all the numbered areas from your main and background fabrics.

For the samples, I sewed a mirrored block (flipped along the vertical) in addition to the original pattern. You can mirror any block to achieve variation in your project designs; just make sure directionality will not be an issue. For example, a block that contains letters will lose its legibility when flipped.

Block Assembly

Seam allowances are ¼″ unless otherwise noted.

Paper piece the feather sections and assemble the block using the following sequence:

A + B   //   C + D   //   AB + CD

FINISHED BLOCK: 3″ × 9″

Construct the Pincushion

1 Lay the backing rectangle and pincushion right sides together. Sew around the edges, leaving 1″–2″ open to turn the pincushion right side out.

2 Fill the pincushion with your filling of choice. I love using crushed walnut shells, which you can usually find in bulk at pet stores (it's reptile bedding). Hand stitch the opening closed.

Tip
FUSSY CUTTING

I fussy cut fabrics for one of the feathers. Remember to hold the pattern up to a light source (or over a lightbox) as you cut to see what part of the fabric will show through!

Fussy-cut plumes

Voodoo Feather Pincushion

Creatures

Many creatures have trademark features that make them difficult to re-create as an artist, a pattern designer, or both. It's hard to get the proportions just right on horses, for instance— and even when you do, it still might look a bit off. So in this chapter, let's tackle whatever it is you think you can't design—if only to show you that you can.

Design Prompt Four
Choose an Animal or Other Object with a Defined (Less Forgiving) Shape

STEP ONE
STUDY YOUR REFERENCE SUBJECT

Of all the prompts in this book, this is probably the one instance where you'll want to truly study images of your subject before embarking on the design process. Fortunately, when it comes to wildlife, there's no shortage of photos documenting the huge variety of species on this planet. So choose one, and read up!

I can't even tell you how many photos of ocean life I combed through before I was comfortable enough to come up with the blocks in My Take (page 78). It doesn't have to be a science, but a little science certainly won't hurt!

STEP TWO **DRAFT YOUR PATTERN**

Given this prompt's parameters, you'll want to follow along closely with the design process in Part II. (See The Design Process, Step Three: Break Up the Reference Subject, page 42.) However, unlike the bud and petals in Part II, you'll likely need a fair number of different sections to get the composition just right. So while it's good to merge areas into a few pieced sections, those small details will make all the difference here.

Tip
WORK FROM GENERAL TO SPECIFIC

That you *might* wind up with more sections doesn't change the fundamentals of the design process. You'll still work from general to specific: Separate your reference subject from the background; then break down the subject into its logical parts, where applicable (for example, legs, body, and head). After you've done this, keep going! Subdivide existing sections or create new ones to capture finer details (hands, hooves) and then even finer ones (hair, fingernails, claws). Remember, it's always a good idea to keep piecing order in mind as you're sketching. That way, you have a general sense of whether dividing an area into even smaller ones will create new sections or work within existing ones. To be sure, tiny areas are a great way to add definition to existing areas—so long as they work with your intended piecing order and don't lead to cumbersome new sections.

STEP THREE **CREATE THE PATTERN**

Once you're happy with the design, make a *mirror copy* of your block, scaling as necessary to your desired final size. Use that copy to create your master pattern. Letter and number the pattern using the method in The Design Process, Step Four: Finalize the Sections and Sequencing (page 47).

MY TAKE // **FOLKSY FRIENDS**

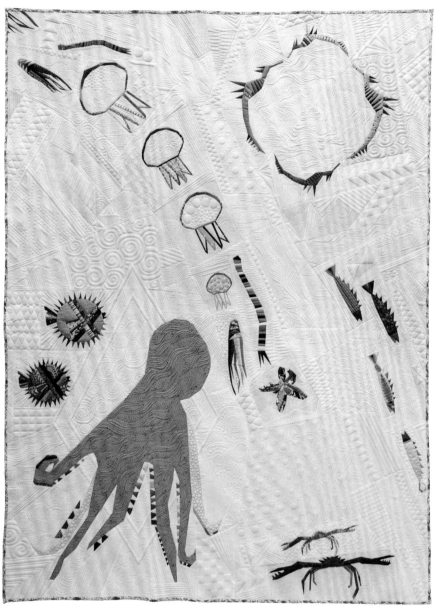

Folksy Friends, 60″ × 80″, quilted by Kathleen Riggins

This is, no doubt, a nod to another one of my favorite subjects—the ocean. As I alluded to earlier, I've spent my entire life trekking across the country to the house where my dad grew up, in a little town just a couple miles from the beach. Summers from my childhood were all about soaking up the sun in my grandmother's backyard, walking to the penny candy store, hunting for crabs in the bay, and steering clear of jellyfish at the beach. And swimming. So much swimming!

Having such fond memories of summers at the ocean, it was inevitable that sea life of some sort would make its way into this book. Enter Folksy Friends: *the second installment of another design of mine titled Folksy Fish.*

Materials

BACKGROUND: 8 yards of assorted low-volume solid fabrics

MAIN: 4 yards of assorted small-cut red/orange fabric and scraps

BACKING: 5 yards

BINDING: ⅝ yard

BATTING: 68″ × 88″

PATTERNS
(pages 125–132)

Cutting

BACKGROUND AND MAIN PAPER-PIECED SECTIONS: Cut enough fabric to cover all the numbered areas from your background and main fabrics.

Block Assembly

Seam allowances are ¼″ unless otherwise noted.

1 This project includes an array of sea life to build your own ocean. Select enough Folksy Friend blocks to cover the approximate-size quilt you want to make.

2 Paper piece the pattern sections of your chosen blocks. (Or, in my case, have your friends help make these friends!)

Tip
WILL I HAVE ENOUGH BLOCKS?

You can always make more blocks as you're working on the layout or add background to fill open spaces.

Skyrocket Seaworm
FINISHED BLOCK: 4″ × 9″

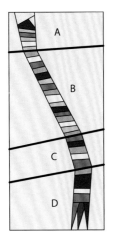

A + B + C + D
The sample includes 2:
1 at 100% and
1 at around 200%.

Macho Minnow
FINISHED BLOCK: 3″ × 9″

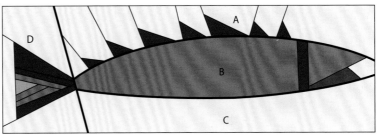

A + B + C
ABC + D
The sample includes 4.

Invisi-Jelly

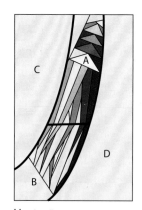

B + C
A + BC

The sample includes 4, ranging in size from 50% to 150%.

Octogoose

FINISHED BLOCK: 6″ × 9″

A + B
AB + C + D

The sample includes 2 full blocks and 1 half-block.

Spike-Tailed Sea Dragon

FINISHED BLOCK: 7″ × 9″

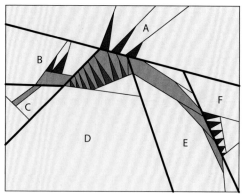

B + C
BC + D + E + F
A + BCDEF

The sample includes 4, ranging in size from 75% to 200%.

Rockstarfish
(also known as Airgui[s]tarfish)

FINISHED BLOCK: 7″ × 9″

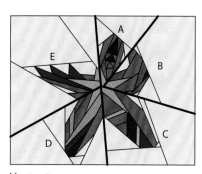

A + B
AB + C
D + E
ABC + DE

The sample includes 1.

Coasting Pincher Crab

FINISHED BLOCK: 4″ × 9″

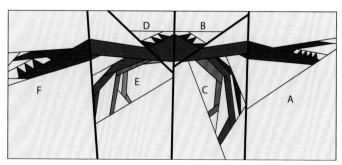

B + C
D + E
A + BC
DE + F
ABC + DEF

The sample includes 2: 1 at 100% and 1 at about 200%.

Pucker-Lipped Puffer Fish

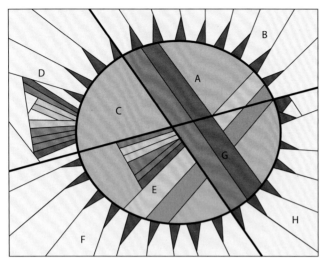

A + B
C + D
E + F
G + H
AB + CD
EF + GH
ABCD + EFGH
The sample includes 2:
1 at 100% and 1 at about 150%.

Tip
FRIENDS LARGE AND SMALL

Don't be afraid to scale up (or down!) the patterns in this book. That's the beauty of whole patterns that omit seam allowances—you can play around with the sizing without the hassle of adjusting seam allowances. For a reminder on how to resize patterns, see Pay Attention to Pattern Scale (page 17).

Septopus

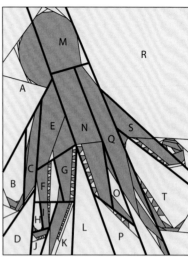

B + C
BC + D
H + I
HI + J
HIJ + K
F + G
HIJK + FG + E + L
BCD + EFGHIJKL + A
N + O
NO + P
NOP + Q
NOPQ + M
ABCDEFGHIJKL + MNOPQ
R + S + T
ABCDEFGHIJKLMNOPQ + RST
The sample includes 1 at about 400%.

Improv Quilt Construction

Believe it or not, I'm not the biggest on improv. I love it when other people do it, but I have always struggled to find my voice within that framework. That is, until I pieced a design (Folksy Fish) that helped me see how I could still be *me* while being—dare I say—"modern?" And you know what? It's growing on me! Sure, it's a big pain when you've got fifteen pieces in obscure shapes that are somehow supposed to fit together ... and no clear path to get there. But on the flip side, you also have full creative control over the process at that same moment. When everything is said and done, you're left with a one-of-a-kind piece. I think that's pretty cool. So rather than stick to the grid for this one, I figured now was as good a time as any to venture back into less charted waters.

STEP ONE PLAN

If you have a designated and available design wall (or other space), you can start placing the blocks as you make them and tweak the layout as you go. If not, you will probably want to piece as many blocks as possible before working on the layout.

For my top, I pieced a number of whole—and half!—sea creatures. Remember the fragments for the edges! Heads, tails, claws, tentacles, and underbellies—everything goes. You can piece them whole then slice them up. Or if you can't stomach the thought of chopping up such harmless little friends, cut the patterns before piecing them instead.

Once I had a few dozen blocks, I sorted them to see how the hues flowed and whether I needed any more in a particular colorway.

STEP TWO ESTABLISH THE TOP ROW

Or the bottom one, in my case. Just pick one edge and go for it. **Fig. A**

I knew I wanted the Septopus octopus to be holding down the fort in the lower left-hand corner of the design. Needless to say, he was the first up on the design wall, followed by a bold duo of Puffer Fish (a veritable face-off indeed!).

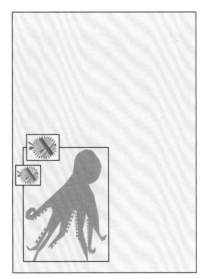

A I started with septopus and some puffer fish toward the bottom of the design.

After setting up that scene, I started to place more sea creatures on my design wall, overlapping each new one with the last until they more than covered my desired width. **Fig. B**

Note: Account for Seam Allowance as You Build

It's important to exceed your desired width by at least several inches. You can always trim later, and you'll lose at least that to seam allowances when you join the blocks.

STEP THREE **WORK YOUR WAY DOWN**

Once you establish the width, you can work your way down (or up) the quilt. **Fig. C**

I recommend intentionally staggering and angling the blocks so that you don't wind up with a pure grid. And don't be afraid to overlap large bits of blocks or leave gaps! **Fig. D**

After you start laying out the blocks, you might decide you want to add more background to give certain species a little more space (or take some away for a more huddled look). You can leave room and revisit those adjustments later, or you can go ahead and add and subtract as you go.

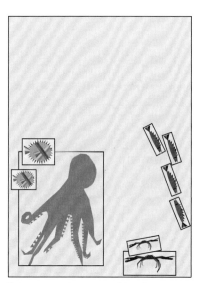

B I scattered more sea friends across the width of the design.

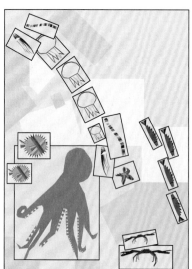

C I used invisi-jellies to work my way up; I added more Folksy Friend blocks and large background pieces, too.

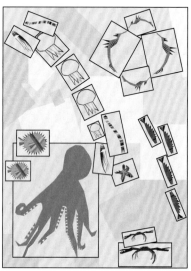

D I added a quartet of spike-tailed sea dragons in the upper right corner.

STEP FOUR ROUND OUT THE DESIGN

Once you're happy with the layout, take a look and determine whether you need to trim significant overlaps or fill in any gaps with leftover background material. **Fig. E**

I have to say, it can be helpful to do the trimming before the filling. Sometimes you can turn right around and use the trimmings to do the filling!

Tip
BEFORE YOU DITCH THOSE BACKGROUND SCRAPS

Keep background scraps or small cuts handy for quick fixes (for example, to fill little gaps of the design wall showing through) now and when you start sewing.

STEP FIVE JOIN THE FRIENDS

As for the assembly itself, once you have a rough layout, what's next is entirely personal. It is improv, after all! So I can tell you my approach, but if it makes no sense to you, go with what does.

What I *will* say is, generally speaking, there are two ways to join your pieced blocks: with straight lines or with gradual curves.

Straight Lines

1 If you're like me, you'll want to pick 2 adjoining blocks that seem like they would go together fairly easily. **Fig. F**

2 Here we have 2 jellyfish. Sew a small strip of background fabric along the bottom of the top jelly; then position it back in place so it overlaps with the jelly below by at least ½″–1″. **Fig. G**

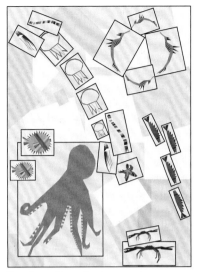

E I placed large background scraps over holes in the background.

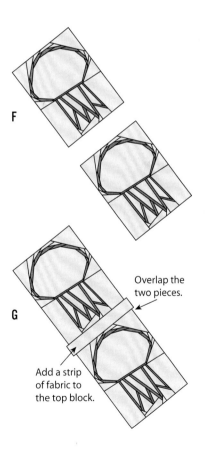

F

G

Overlap the two pieces.

Add a strip of fabric to the top block.

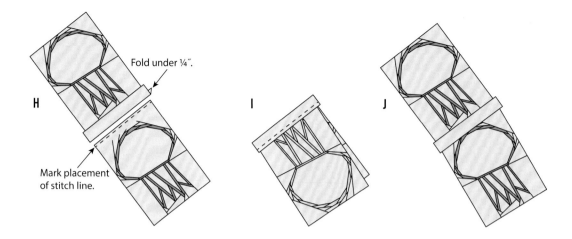

Fold under ¼″.

H

Mark placement
of stitch line.

I

J

3 Tuck under ¼″ of the top jellyfish and crease that straight line. Lightly mark the bottom block along the same line you just creased into the top one—this will be your seamline for sewing the 2 blocks together. **Fig. H**

4 Carefully flip the top block onto the bottom one, right sides together, before removing your blocks from the layout. You're going to line up the crease on the top block and the marked line on the bottom block. Sew together along the crease. Press to ensure the seam lies flat before trimming your seam allowance to ¼″. **Figs. I & J**

Note: Press!
Really. Press! This is pretty important—so important I'm saying it twice. *So long as you press as you go, you're verifying that your top will lie flat. And if there's slack in a particular joint, you can press a fold to remove it and sew along that pressed fold so the top lies flat.*

5 Place the 2-block unit back onto the design space, and figure out where to go next. I like to continue the quest for low-lying fruit (joints that appear to be fairly straightforward) because it boosts my confidence before getting into what-have-I-gotten-myself-into territory—the proverbial eye of the hurricane, I suppose! At the same time, I don't like to piece units too large at first because it's more difficult, in my opinion, to join large irregular units to other large irregular units.

6 If you find yourself at a standstill, you can always add background to straighten out or square off otherwise uneven edges and join sections along those newly straightened edges.

Gradual Curves

One of my favorite tricks is to overlap two pieces you want to join and cut a gradual curve through both pieces to establish your sew line. This can be especially helpful when you reach a breaking point and can't figure out how you're *possibly* going to join two pieces together with straight lines. Enter this quick, gradual-curve fix!

1 Place both pieces on a cutting mat, making sure they overlap by at least 1″–2″ along the edges you want to join. **Fig. K**

2 Using a rotary cutter, cut freehand a gradual curve in the overlapped area so that you are cutting through both pieces. **Fig. L**

3 Carefully remove the scraps from the cut so that you are left with the 2 pieces interlocking side by side (like yin and yang). **Fig. M**

4 Create small registration marks using a fabric-safe pen. **Fig. N**

5 Pin the pieces, right sides together, along those marks.

6 Slowly sew the pieces together using a standard stitch length and ¼″ seam allowance. Take care to realign the edges if they shift.

7 Press.

Finishing

Once you're happy with the top, piece the backing. Layer the backing, batting, and quilt top; quilt; and bind as desired.

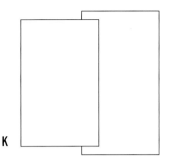

K

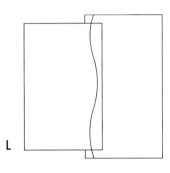

L

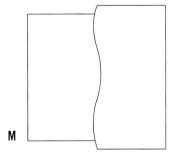

M

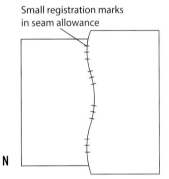

Small registration marks in seam allowance

N

Think Outside the (Square) Block

Not all good things come in square packages! In this chapter, you'll have some fun getting outside your four-sided comfort zone to see what you can create within new, non-rectangular bounds.

Design Prompt Five

Choose a Familiar Shape to Create a New, Non-Square Block that Interlocks upon Repeat

Work with hexagons, diamonds, or triangles, for example, or a group of shapes. Then design a pattern within that shape.

STEP ONE **TRACE THE SHAPE**

Begin by tracing the shape on letter-size (or larger) paper. Make a couple of copies if you're designing right on that paper; otherwise, have a few sheets of tracing paper on hand.

STEP TWO **GET INSPIRED**

Think about how the shape inspires you. Or if that seems like putting the cart before the horse, find your inspiration first and then figure out how it might fit within a non-square frame.

STEP THREE **DRAFT YOUR PATTERN**

Whether the block shape inspired its contents or vice versa, start sketching once that inspiration strikes!

STEP FOUR **CREATE YOUR PATTERN**

Once you're happy with the design, make a *mirror copy* of your block, scaling as necessary to your desired final size. Use that copy to create your master pattern. Letter and number the pattern using the method in The Design Process, Step Four: Finalize the Sections and Sequencing (page 47).

Note: A Practical Note About Complex, Multi-Section Designs

Keep in mind one design reality: More section lines equal more seamlines, which could result in very slight variations on the shape of the block once all those sections are sewn together. (To be fair, this is true no matter the block shape, but it can be problematic in this exercise because this design is premised on a shape repeating seamlessly.)

For instance, a 7″ hexagon pattern made up of 22 odd-shaped sections will not be a perfect 7″ hexagon after sewing all 22 sections together. It won't be off much—maybe a fraction of an inch. But this will directly affect the accuracy of your repeat, and things might not line up. If complexity is still your thing (guilty!) and accuracy is, too (eh … not so much), try to keep important design elements more than ¼″–½″ away from the finished block edge. That way, you will be able to trim your pieced blocks to size for more accurate quilt top construction without having to worry about losing prominent design details in the seam allowance. (Use an unpieced pattern, with seam allowance added, to trim finished blocks.)

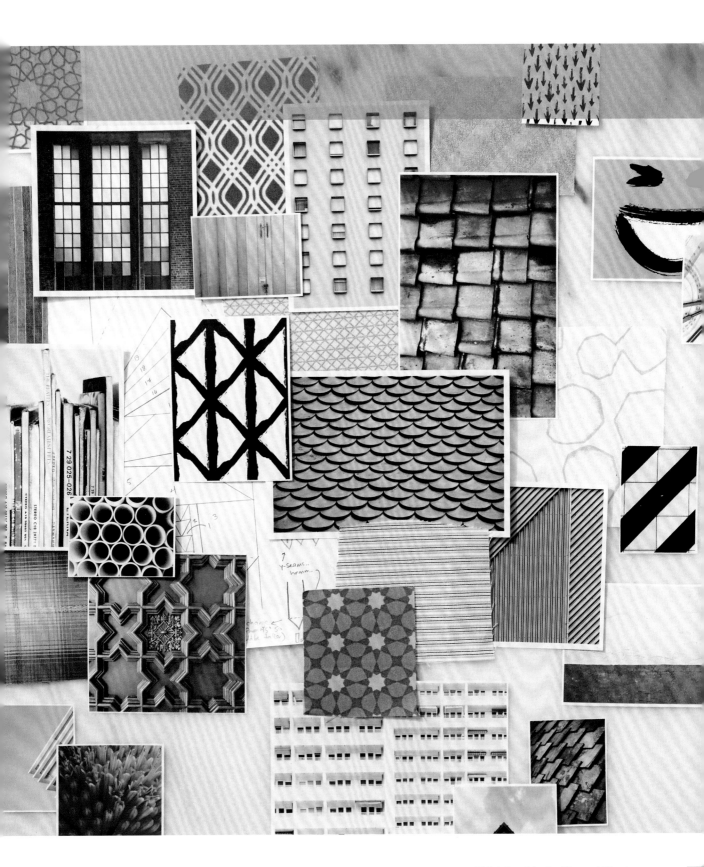

MY TAKE // **FIREFLIES**

Fireflies, 36″ × 48″, quilted by Rachael Dorr

There's something so magical about fireflies; I think that rings true for most people. I remember summers as a kid when I would chase after them on my grandmother's lawn, and now I love seeing my daughters' eyes light up as they do the same.

Full disclosure: When I first proposed this chapter, I had a tree quilt in mind. I wanted to use alternating rows of triangles and elongated rectangles to create a staggered forest of quirky-patterned evergreens. But then I decided to stitch up all the projects in color order, with this chapter falling in the orange/yellow section of the color wheel. As you likely guessed, a forest blaze wasn't exactly the quaint scene I'd envisioned during the proposal process! Enter the triangular fireflies—harmless little twinkling lights whose oranges and yellows evoke nostalgic summer nights (and, importantly, not wildfires*!).*

Materials

BACKGROUND: 2½ yards of assorted white or low-volume fabrics

MAIN: 1 yard of assorted yellow and orange fabric scraps or small cuts

BACKING: 1⅝ yards (if 44″ wide) or 2½ yards (if less than 44″ wide)

BINDING: ½ yard

BATTING: 44″ × 56″

PATTERNS (pages 133–137)

Cutting

BACKGROUND: Cut at least 12 strips 7½″ × width of fabric from the background.

BACKGROUND AND MAIN PAPER-PIECED SECTIONS: Cut enough fabric to cover all the numbered areas from your background and main fabrics. Repeat until you have enough pieces to make as many different fireflies as your heart desires. I made 5 (one of each design).

BINDING: Cut 6 strips 2½″ × width of fabric.

Block Assembly

Seam allowances are ¼″ unless otherwise noted.

1 This project features 5 different firefly designs, each a little different than the next. Select whichever ones you want flickering across your quilt.

2 Paper piece the firefly sections and assemble the blocks using the following piecing sequences. Each finished block is a 7″-tall equilateral triangle (side length is 8.083″).

Firefly 1
B + C + D
BCD + A

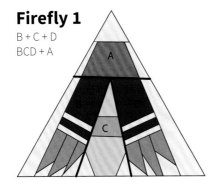

Firefly 2
A + B + C

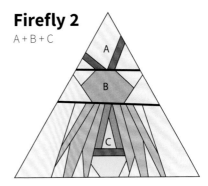

Firefly 3
B + C
D + E
BC + DE
BCDE + A

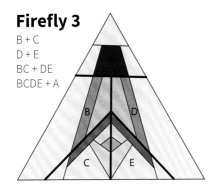

Firefly 4
B + C
BC + A

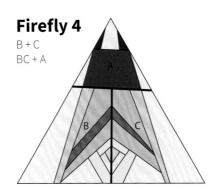

Firefly 5
B + C
BC + A

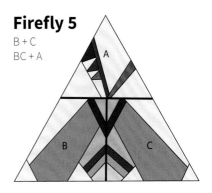

Improv Quilt Construction

1 Scatter your fireflies on your design wall (or floor). No matter which direction the bugs are flying, just make sure all the *triangles* are oriented along the same grid so you can easily assemble them. Rotate any wayward fireflies into alignment so that all the bugs are flying in the same plane to avoid improv assembly. **Fig. A**

2 Fill in the background with the 7½″ × width of fabric strips until your desired quilt area is covered. **Fig. B**

Note: Alternative Layout

In place of the 7½″ strips, you can also use 7½″ unfinished equilateral triangles from a variety of low-volume prints for a flickering background. Just skip Step 3, and resume at Step 4 by sewing the triangles and fireflies in each row together before joining the rows into a top.

3 Where each strip joins a firefly, cut that strip at a 60° angle (the same as an equilateral triangle), taking care to leave at least a ¼″ seam allowance for the joint. **Fig. C**

4 Sew the strips and fireflies in each row together. **Fig. D**

5 Starting in one corner, piece the diagonal rows together into the top. Trim to your desired finished size.

Finishing

Piece the backing. Layer the backing, batting, and quilt top; quilt; and bind as desired.

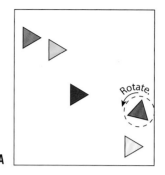

A

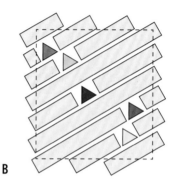

B

C

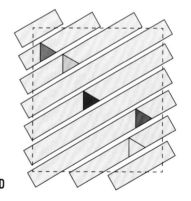

D

Repeat Designs

I took a fabric design class, thinking it would be a fun way to spend a day. Little did I know I would be totally mesmerized by the way repeats come together. Much like foundation paper piecing, each new repeat is like its own puzzle just waiting to be worked out. Who knew drawing could be so much fun? After my class ended, a friend of mine commented that even if my drawings didn't make their way onto fabric, it would be cool to use them as inspiration for a future quilt. I stared (and stared) at the repeats I'd drawn during class, trying to figure out how in the world I could translate them into a quilt design. Then, as I was holding just the single repeat, it struck me—I was staring the block right in the face. After this exercise, you will be, too!

Crash Course in Repeats

BASIC REPEAT

A basic repeat is tiled straight up and down, left and right, in straight columns and rows. To practice a basic repeat, use four sheets of paper to form one large repeat.

 Tape 4 sheets of paper together to form 1 large sheet. This combined sheet will become a single repeat.

Tip

WHAT SIZE PAPER?

I used 7˝ × 9˝ pages—that is, the printable space for this book—but you can use any size you'd like. To get the concept down, I recommend using a slightly *smaller* paper size (standard letter-size paper folded in quarters will do the trick!). You'll find that more compact papers will be less cumbersome as you're getting started, plus it won't take much time to fill with your designs!

2 Flip the combined sheet over so the taped side is down, and lightly mark a number in each corner, as shown. **Fig. A**

A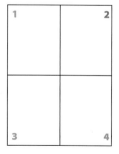

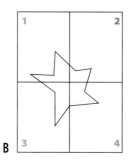
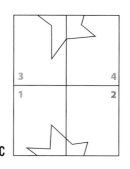
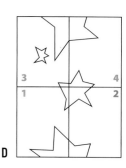

B   C   D

3 Start drawing your design in the center of the paper, taking care not to touch any of the outer edges of the combined sheet. **Fig. B**

Tip

DO I HAVE TO DRAW OUTLINES?

For this example, I'm drawing outlines of stars using straight lines. You do not have to use outlines or exclusively straight lines, but that will make things a little easier when you go to convert your repeat into a paper-piecing pattern. If you would rather fill in your repeat to create a more robust reference, go for it!

4 Cut the combined sheet in half horizontally. Switch the top and bottom halves; then tape the pages back together on the back. **Fig. C**

5 Draw more, again staying within the edges of your paper. **Fig. D**

6 Cut the sheet in half vertically. Switch the halves and tape them back together on the back. **Fig. E**

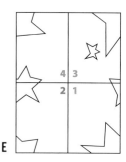

E

7 Fill in any gaps with additional details, taking care not to touch the outside edges. **Fig. F**

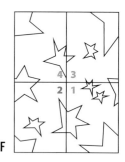

F

Tip

YOU CAN DRAW OVER THE NUMBERS

Remember, the numbers are just there for your reference—not as part of the design—so you can draw over some or all of them at any time. Otherwise, you will wind up with four gaps in your design where each number was written.

8 Test the repeat. There are a couple ways to go about this. If you have a copier handy, the easiest way is to make multiple copies of your design and tile them on a grid (remember, straight columns and rows). Another (slower) way is to take an oversize sheet of tracing paper—at least 6 times larger than your combined sheet—and trace the design multiple times to see how the pattern develops. **Fig. G**

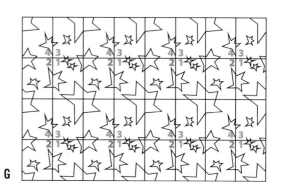

G

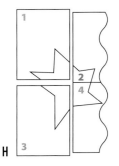
H

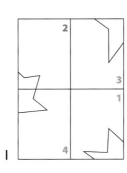
I

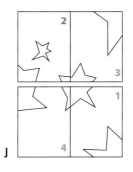
J

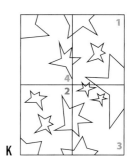
K

HALF-DROP REPEATS

Half-drop repeats are like basic repeats, but the design staggers a half step vertically. Like a staircase, the design takes one step down each time it repeats.

1 Follow Basic Repeat, Steps 1–3 (pages 94–96).

2 Cut the combined sheet in half vertically.

3 After cutting the combined sheet in half vertically, cut the sheet containing pages 1 and 3 in half horizontally. **Fig. H**

4 Switch pages 1 and 3, and tape those 2 pages back together on the back. Switch the left and right halves and tape them together, as shown. **Fig. I**

5 Draw more, again staying within the edges of your paper. Cut the sheet in half horizontally. **Fig. J**

6 Switch the halves, and tape them back together on the back. Fill in any gaps with additional details, taking care not to touch the outer edges. **Fig. K**

7 Test the repeat to see what pattern emerges by making photocopies or tracing by hand (see Basic Repeat, Step 8, previous page). **Fig. L**

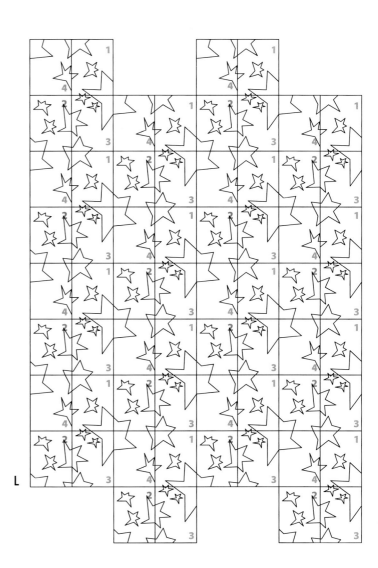
L

Design Prompt Six

Create a Block Repeat Using Surface Pattern Design Techniques

Once you have your repeat, *that* will be the starting point for designing your paper-piecing pattern for this exercise. Whether you choose to do a basic repeat or a half-drop, the end result will be four blocks (1–4) that, when laid out just right, will create a quilt pattern unlike anything you've seen before.

STEP ONE DOODLE!

Following the crash course (page 94), choose a repeat style, tape your papers, and start drawing. Then cut, tape, and draw some more until you've found a quilt-worthy repeat.

STEP TWO MARK THE ENTRY/EXIT POINTS ALONG THE EDGES

To maximize the seamless effect of your finished design, you'll want to pay very close attention to the parts that cross over from one page to the next—otherwise, your repeat could be slightly off. You want to mark each point where the design leaves the page.

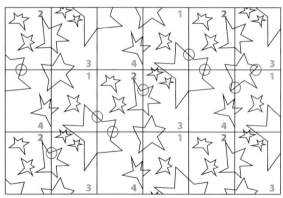

Using the half-drop star repeat from earlier, here are some of the points to flag before you draft the pattern to ensure the assembled block is as seamless as your sketch.

Once you've done that, test the repeat to make sure you've got the markings right. Make multiple copies and lay them out in the sequence described in the crash course (tiled straight for basic repeats, page 96, or staggered for half-drops, page 97).

STEP THREE DRAFT YOUR PATTERN

Break down the pattern, just as you did with the echinacea plant in The Design Process (page 39). While most of the design elements *within* each of the four repeat sections will be subject to your artistic interpretation, the one nonnegotiable will be the entry/exit points you just marked. Those important points must remain in the exact same spots to ensure a truly seamless repeat.

STEP FOUR CREATE YOUR PATTERN

Once you're happy with the design, make a *mirror copy* of your block, scaling as necessary to your desired final size. Use that copy to create your master pattern. Letter and number the pattern using the method in The Design Process, Step Four: Finalize the Sections and Sequencing (page 47).

MY TAKE // **JUNGLEVIEW**

Jungleview, 28″ × 36″

If Plant Lady *didn't give it away by now, I have this thing with plants. (To be fair, in the warm months our house is surrounded by greenery, so those leafy-green givers just feel like home.) Since taking that fabric design workshop, I also have this thing with repeats. So when it came time to prepare a repeat in a vibrant yellow-green colorway, it only made sense to combine my love of the two. To develop this half-drop repeat, I swapped the stars in the crash course (page 94) for leaves. I drew a single monstera leaf, rearranged the pages to add the next, and repeated that process until the jungle canopy that was stuck in my head was finally down on paper.*

Materials

BACKGROUND: 2 yards of assorted white or low-volume fabrics

MAIN: 2 yards of assorted yellow, green, and aqua fabrics

BACKING: 1 yard

BINDING: ⅜ yard

BATTING: 36″ × 44″

PATTERNS (pages 138–141)

Cutting

BACKGROUND AND MAIN PAPER-PIECED SECTIONS: Cut enough fabric to cover all the numbered areas from your background and main fabrics. Repeat until you have enough pieces to make 4 each of blocks 1–4.

BINDING: Cut 4 strips 2½″ × width of fabric.

Block Assembly

Seam allowances are ¼″ unless otherwise noted.

Paper piece the block sections and assemble the blocks using the following piecing sequences. Each finished block measures 14″ × 18″.

Quadrant 1

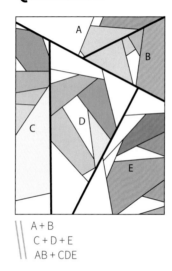

‖ A + B
‖ C + D + E
‖ AB + CDE

Quadrant 2

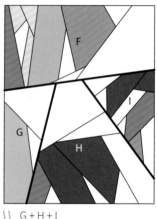

‖ G + H + I
‖ F + GHI

Quadrant 3

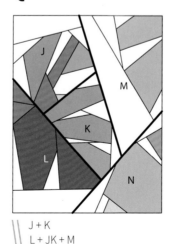

‖ J + K
‖ L + JK + M
‖ JKLM + N

Quadrant 4

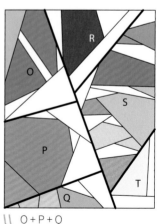

‖ O + P + Q
‖ R + S + T
‖ OPQ + RST

Quilt Construction

1 Lay out the blocks in sequence, as shown. As discussed in Crash Course in Repeats (page 94), half-drop repeats align in a staggered fashion. So if you think of pages 1–4 as a single unit, this design is really made up of a few staggered repeats, like the stars in Half-Drop Repeats (page 97). **Fig. A**

A

2	1	4	3
4	3	2	1
2	1	4	3
4	3	2	1

2 Sew the blocks into rows. Press.

B

Note: Matching Points Across Pattern Pages
Using pins, match up the points where the pattern crosses from one page to the next. This will help make your repeat as seamless as possible. **Fig. B**

3 Sew the rows together into the top. Press.

Finishing

Piece the backing. Layer the backing, batting, and quilt top; quilt; and bind as desired.

Single Foundation Paper Piecing

I can't take credit for this, but I've been itching to incorporate it into my work ever since stumbling upon Jamie Swanson's use of the method (Jamie credits Teri at Making Miniature Quilts for the idea). Regardless of who originally thought of it, I'm officially spreading the word as a tiny-paper-piecing aficionado!

Single foundation paper piecing is a technique that involves laying out patterns on a single page to facilitate easier piecing and assembly where point matching is critical. But let's be clear up front—you can't do this with just any pattern. For simplicity's sake, let's assume you can use this method only for symmetrical designs that repeat in the round (for example, squares or rectangles with a 90° angle and triangles or wedges with a 45° angle)—so basically a kaleidoscope. There may be other suitable designs, but let's not get ahead of ourselves!

Crash Course in Single Foundation Paper Piecing

The good news is that creating a single-paper foundation is easier than it sounds.

1 Design the original shape, the one that will repeat in the round. This can be a square, rectangle, right triangle, or wedge; however, it must be a *single* section (that is, one that can be pieced continuously without any breaks). **Fig. A**

2 Once you have that, make enough copies to repeat 360°: for example, 4 squares or 8 wedges 45°. Lay out the blocks as they would appear in final form on a piece of grid paper so all the section lines are adjacent to one another. **Fig. B**

3 Add a uniform gap between all sections. The minimum gap is 1″ to account for seam allowances, but 2″ will also work.

Note: Stay Locked into the Grid
The most important part of this entire process is ensuring that the gap is as exact as possible. All horizontal and vertical section edges should be on the same plane, with a buffer space between them. Use a ruler and the grid lines to double-check that everything lines up.

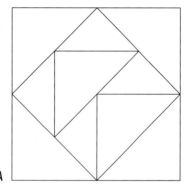

A

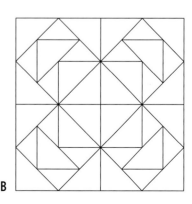

B

4 Tape the pattern pieces in place. Draw a vertical line and a horizontal line exactly halfway between the respective halves. **Fig. C**

5 Copy the pattern, cut out *the combined unit*, and remove the square where the gaps intersect. **Fig D**

To join the pieced sections, fold along either the horizontal or vertical line so that your sections are sandwiched right sides together. Sew along the section edges running parallel to the fold. Unfold and repeat with the other line; then remove the papers and press.

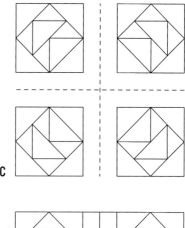

C

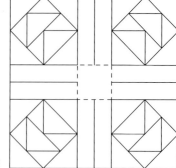

D

Design Prompt Seven

Create a Geometric Design that Repeats in the Round to Form the Complete Pattern

That is, work with wedges of a circle or right triangles within a square.

STEP ONE **DRAFT YOUR DESIGN**

This can be as simple or complex as your heart desires. Just remember, each unit must be one section—otherwise you'd have to cut them apart, which would defeat the underlying purpose of this method.

Note: Except …

Okay, technically you can *have multiple sections, as you'll see in My Take (next page). But those sections must join at a right angle that is parallel to either the horizontal or vertical line in the gaps. And that just makes things sound more complicated than they need to be. So for now, let's just go with single-section units.*

STEP TWO **ASSEMBLE THE PATTERN SECTIONS ON A SINGLE SHEET**

The trick with single foundation paper piecing is getting everything on one piece of paper so that it's a matter of folding the paper to get the alignment just right rather than trying to line up teeny tiny patterns. Follow along with the steps outlined in Crash Course in Single Foundation Paper Piecing (page 102) to arrange your patterns on a single page.

STEP THREE **CREATE YOUR PATTERN**

Once you're happy with the design, copy and scale your pattern to your desired finished size. Use that copy to create your master pattern. Letter and number the pattern using the method in The Design Process, Step Four: Finalize the Sections and Sequencing (page 47).

MY TAKE // **DOUBLE DIAMOND WEDDING RING**

Double Diamond Wedding Ring, 56″ × 56″, quilted by Andrea Munro of Practical Dazzle

Some of you may recall a double wedding ring (DWR) quilt that won Best in Show several years ago at QuiltCon. Afterward, the maker of that award-winning beauty hosted a DWR challenge, inviting all quilters to create a double wedding ring quilt. Somewhere in between studying for the bar and basking in the glory of my last summer as a student, I came up with a design that featured round-cut diamonds at each intersection in place of the cornerstones typically found in DWR quilts. Here, I've toned it down a notch, adding just a few select pieces of bling and keeping the simple square cornerstones in the rest.

Materials

BACKGROUND: 2¼ yards of white or low-volume fabric

DIAMONDS: 1 yard of assorted gray fabrics—at least 8 monochromatic fabrics in a range of values

MAIN: 4 yards of assorted green, aqua, and blue fabrics

BACKING: 3½ yards

BINDING: ⅝ yard

BATTING: 62″ × 62″

PATTERNS (pages 142 and 143)

Cutting

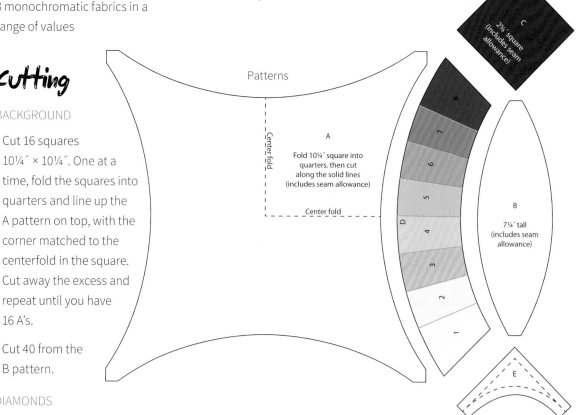

Patterns

BACKGROUND

- Cut 16 squares 10¼″ × 10¼″. One at a time, fold the squares into quarters and line up the A pattern on top, with the corner matched to the centerfold in the square. Cut away the excess and repeat until you have 16 A's.

- Cut 40 from the B pattern.

DIAMONDS

- Cut enough fabric to cover all the numbered areas from your assorted grays. Repeat until you have enough to make 12 of each single-paper pattern F (3 complete diamonds).

MAIN

- Cut 68 C squares 2⅝″ × 2⅝″.

- Cut 12 lighter fabrics from the E pattern (the outer curve to set the diamonds).

- Cut enough fabric to cover all the numbered areas on pattern D from your foreground colors.

  Specifically, you will need:

  480 pieces of fabric to cover areas 2–7, which are identical

  80 pieces for area 1

  80 pieces for area 8

BINDING

- Cut 7 strips 2½″ × width of fabric.

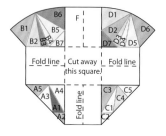

Note

I chose to finish my sample quilt by trimming off the outer curves, but the instructions here will result in a traditional wedding ring, with two arcs all the way around and a curved outer edge.

Block Assembly

Seam allowances are ¼″ unless otherwise noted.

MAKE THE BLING

1 When you cut out the single-paper foundation, *do not cut out each lettered section* as you would with any other design! Instead, cut out the entire pattern (which resembles a shield), and then cut away the inner square. (Removing that square will allow you to fold and sew the pattern sections together as a single unit.) For each diamond, you will need 4 single-paper units (each is one-quarter of the gemstone).

2 To make your diamonds sparkle, sort your fabrics by value, dark to light. Then consider the following as you plan your design:

- Focus darker fabrics in sections pointed toward the outer edge.

- Within the same wedge, avoid using the same fabric in adjacent sections.

- Be mindful of fabric used along the radius so you don't wind up with the same shades next to one another when you start assembling the eighths into quarters. (For example, use different fabrics in B2 and A5 of the F pattern because they will eventually be joined.)

- Still, mix it up! Randomness is your friend here and will result in more sparkle (**Fig. A**). Rather than trying to plan too much, I put all my pieces in a dish and randomly picked the next one (like drawing a name out of hat!).

Tip
ASSEMBLY-LINE PIECING

Since you'll need four of the sample pattern for each diamond, now is a great time to piece in an assembly-line fashion as described in Assembly-Line Paper Piecing (page 22).

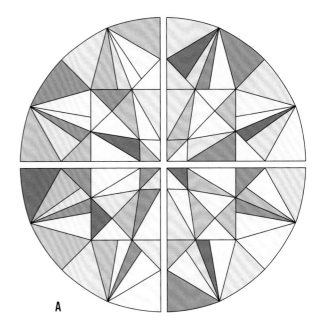

A

3 Paper piece the diamond sections (A–D, as noted on the F pattern) one at a time.

4 Fold along the horizontal line so the pieced sections are right sides together. (If any seam allowance extends into the crease, trim it down to a rough ¼″; then refold.) Sew the continuous line that separates A from B and C from D.

5 Unfold the unit and fold the vertical line. Sew along the continuous line that separates B from D and A from C. Make 12.

6 Remove the papers and press.

7 Sew E to the diamond quarter-unit. Repeat until you have 12. Press and trim each to 2⅝″ × 2⅝″. See Curved Piecing: Tin Can Sprig (page 30). **Fig. B**

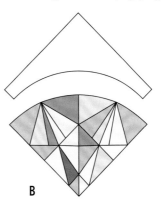

B

PAPER PIECE THE ARCS

In the interest of full disclosure, the D arcs can be pieced using traditional template patterns. Areas 2–7 are the exact same shape, and area 1 is a mirror copy of area 8. However, since this is a book about *foundation paper piecing*, it seemed appropriate to make the arc section a paper-pieced unit, too. Paper piece the D arcs. Make 80.

A

Tip

HOW TO NOT PAPER PIECE THE ARCS

If you'd rather piece the arcs using traditional template patterns, trace areas 1, 2, and 8 onto a piece of paper. Using a ruler with a ¼″ guide, add a seam allowance to each. Cut your main fabrics from those patterns. To assemble, sew 6 piece 2s together to form the main arc; then add piece 1 and 8 to either end.

Note: Planning the Layout

If you haven't already, now is a perfect time to start planning the layout. For starters, you'll want to determine which three intersections should host the diamonds. If you aren't going for an overall scrappy layout, it helps to see all the arcs up before you start joining them together.

B

PIECE THE MELONS

1 The melons are the 2 D arcs joined together by the B oval-shaped background piece. Sew 1 arc to 1 B. **Fig. A**

2 Sew 2 C squares to each end of a second arc. Remember, 12 of these squares will contain one-quarter of your diamond units. **Fig. B**

3 Sew the second arc to the D/B unit. Make 40. **Fig. C**

C

Quilt Construction

1 Lay out all the A shapes in grid of 4 across and 4 down.

2 Lay out the melon pieces, filling in the spaces between the A shapes. **Fig. A**

3 Piece the blocks into horizontal rows, using all the vertical melons in each row to join the A sections. Press. You should now have 4 wavelike rows separated by horizontal melons. **Fig. B**

A

B

4 In the top row, piece the 4 horizontal melons *on top* in place. Press. **Fig. C**

5 Piece the first and third horizontal melon to the bottom of the first row. **Fig. D**

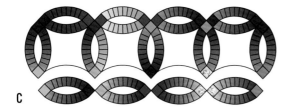

C

D

6 Piece the second and fourth horizontal melons to the top of the second row. **Fig. E**

7 Continue this pattern until all the melons are joined to a row. Join all the horizontal melons to the bottom of the last row. **Fig. F**

8 Piece the rows together as shown, following the S curves, to create the top. **Fig. G**

9 Keep the curved perimeter, or trim the outer arcs to square off the design for an edgier look.

E

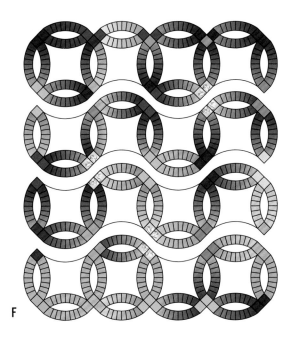

F

G

Finishing

Piece the backing. Layer the backing, batting, and quilt top; quilt; and bind as desired.

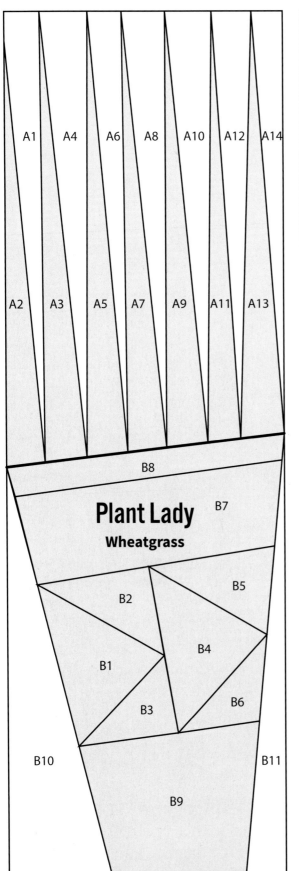

Plant Lady

Wheatgrass

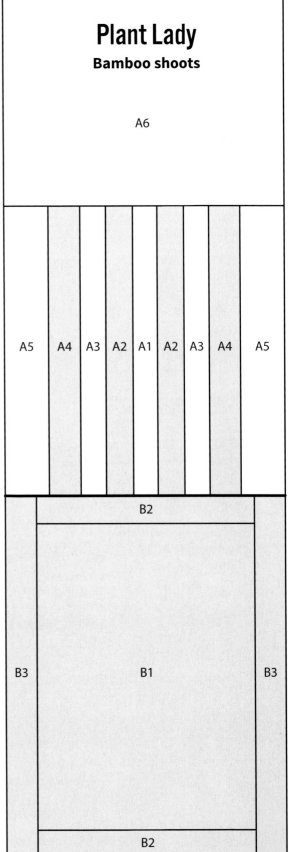

Plant Lady

Bamboo shoots

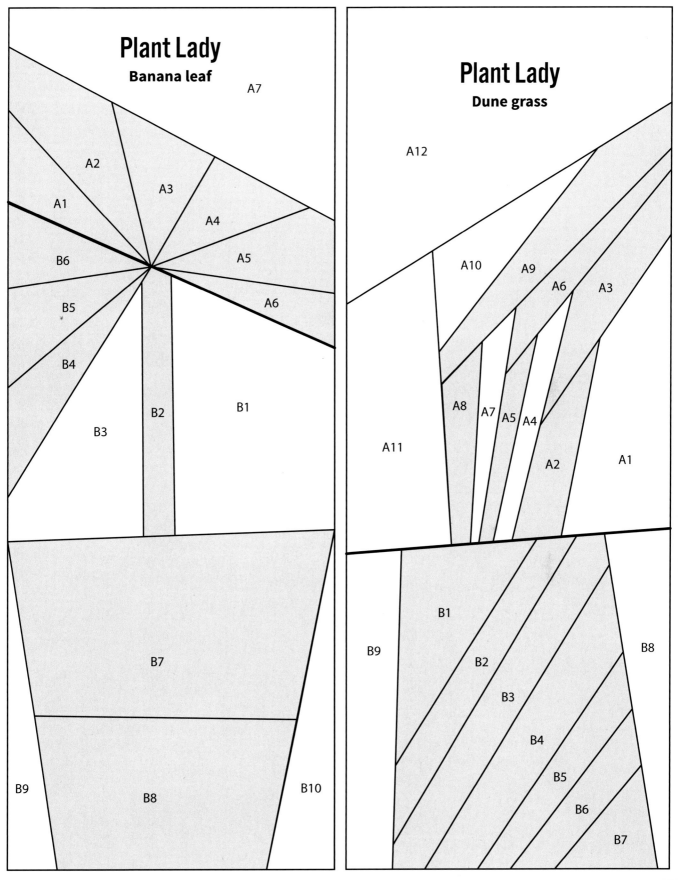

Plant Lady
Banana leaf

Plant Lady
Dune grass

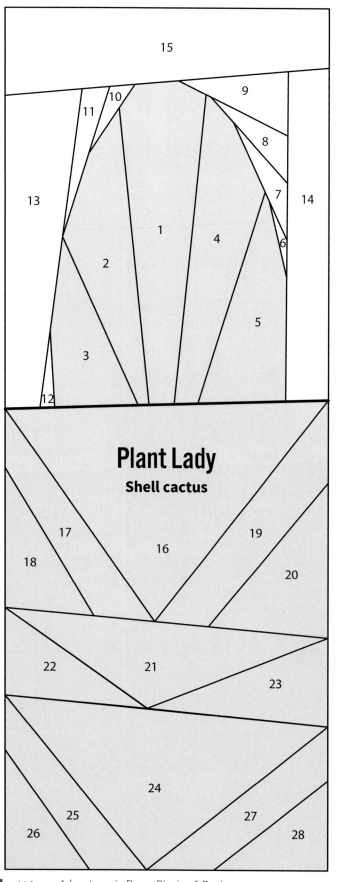

Plant Lady
Shell cactus

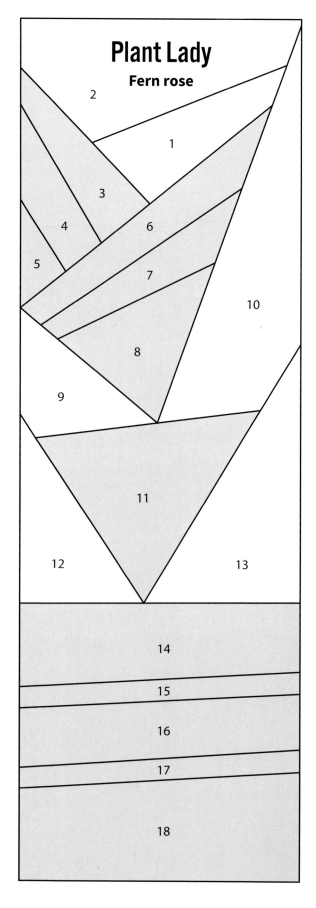

Plant Lady
Fern rose

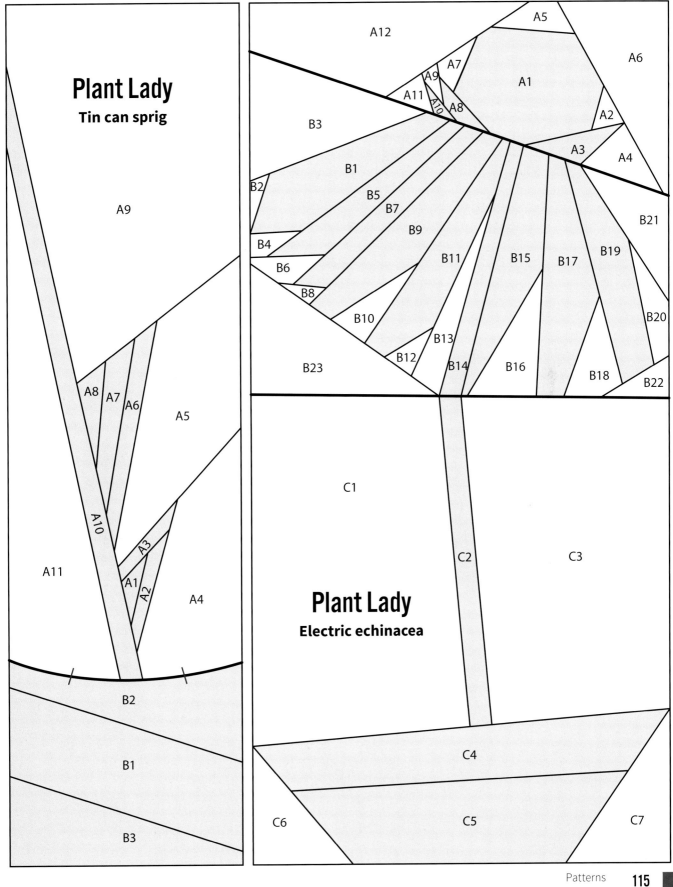

Plant Lady
Tin can sprig

Plant Lady
Electric echinacea

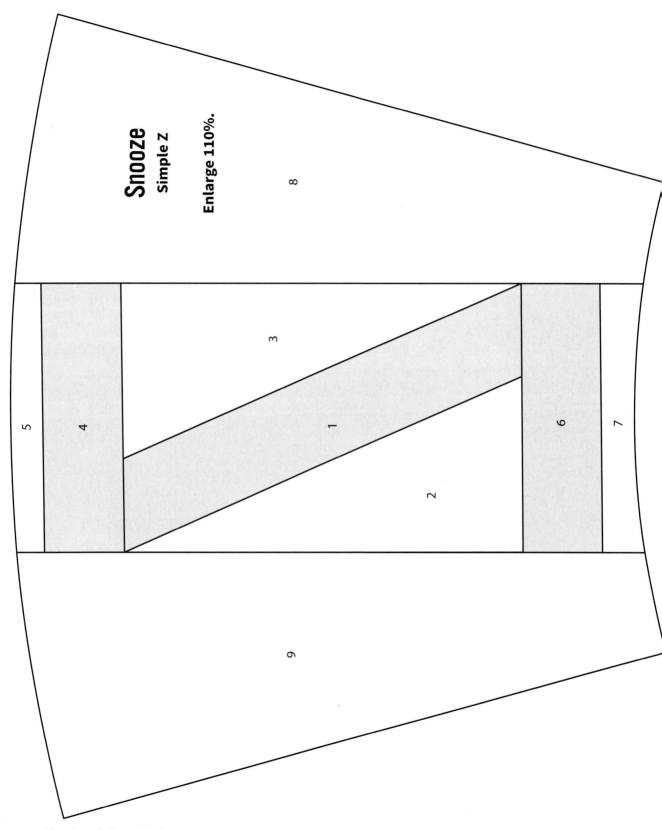

Snooze
Simple Z

Enlarge 110%.

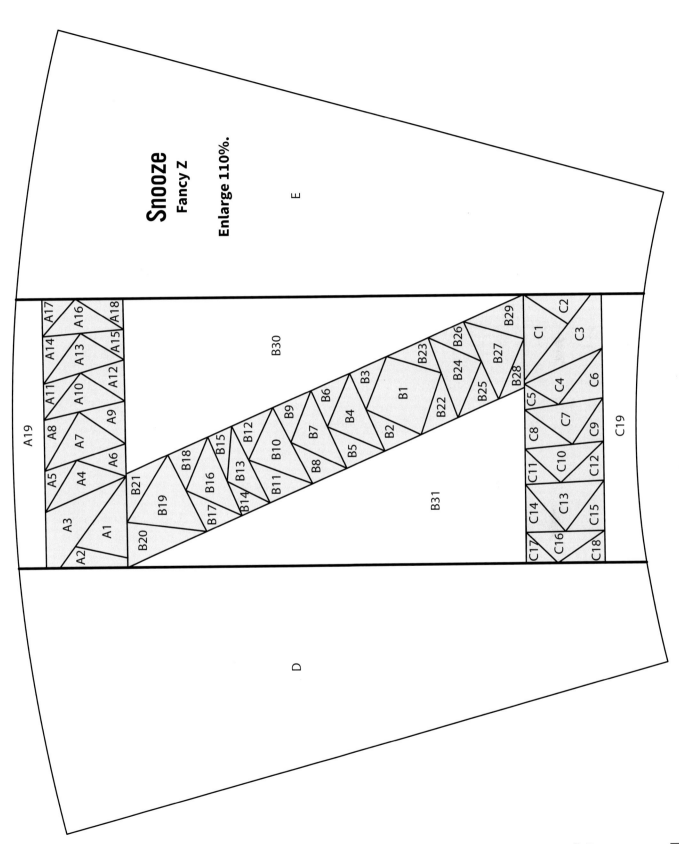

Snooze
Fancy Z

Enlarge 110%.

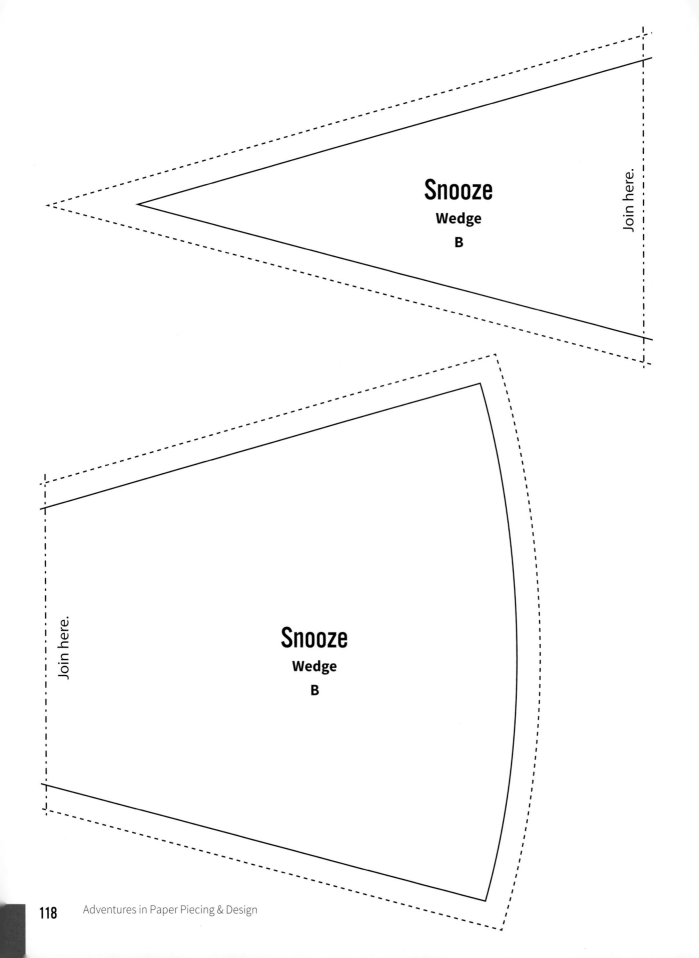

Snooze

Wedge

B

Join here.

Snooze

Wedge

B

Join here.

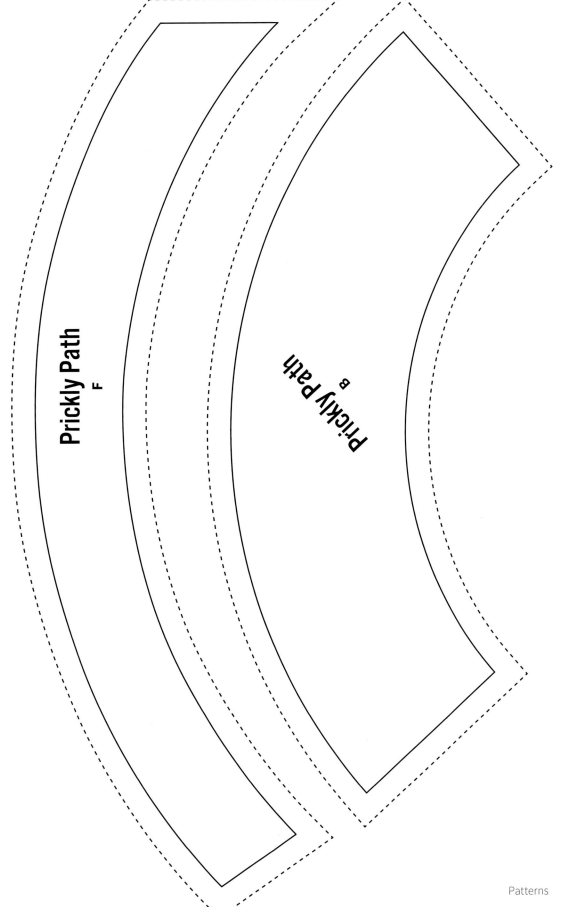

Prickly Path
F

Prickly Path
B

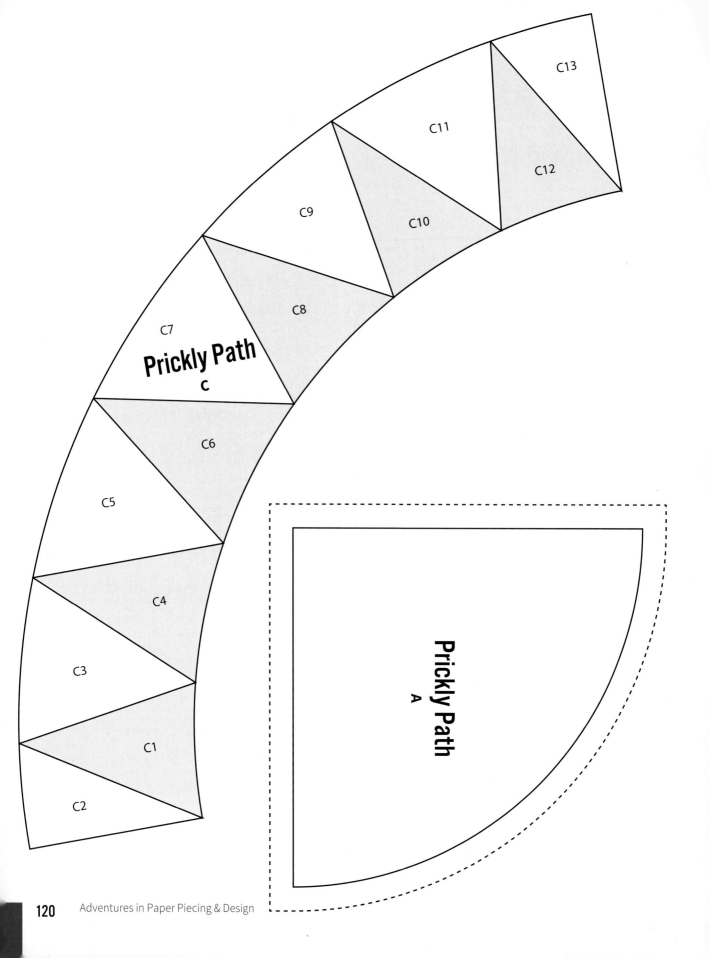

C13

C11

C12

C9

C10

C7

Prickly Path
C

C8

C6

C5

C4

C3

C1

C2

Prickly Path
A

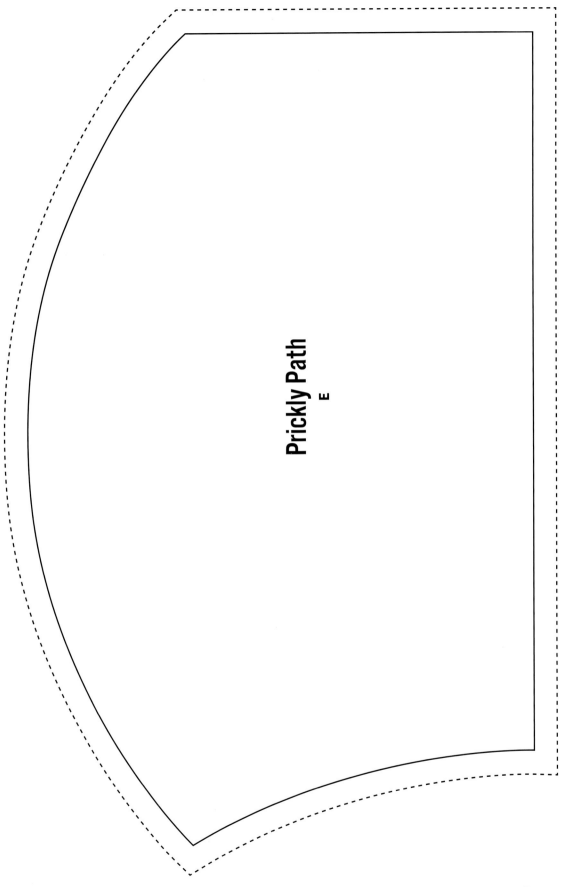

Prickly Path
E

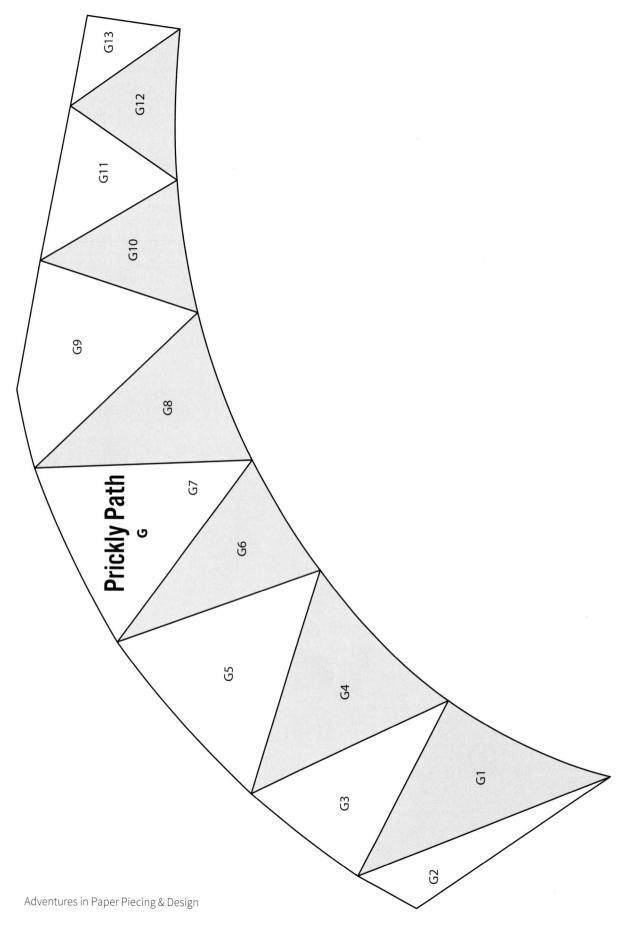

Prickly Path
G

G13
G12
G11
G10
G9
G8
G7
G6
G5
G4
G3
G1
G2

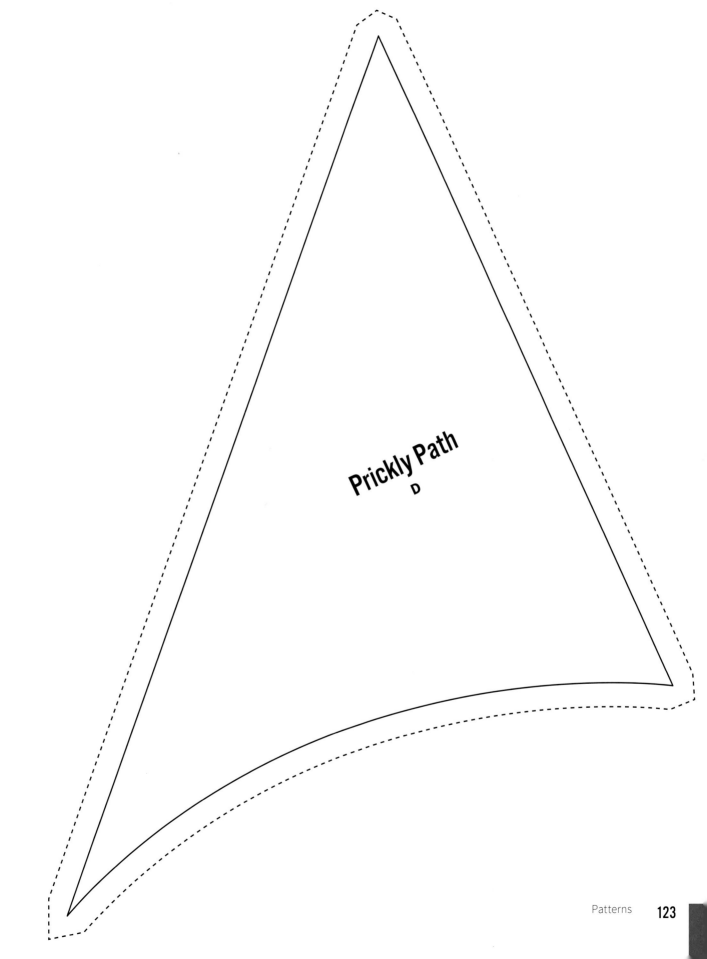

Prickly Path
D

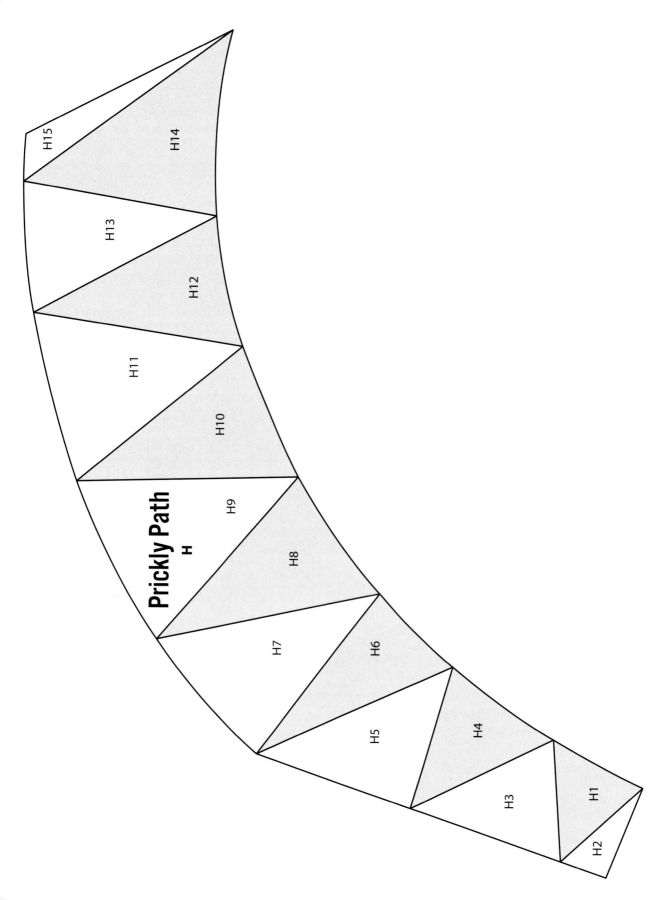

Prickly Path

H

H15

H14

H13

H12

H11

H10

H9

H8

H7

H6

H5

H4

H3

H1

H2

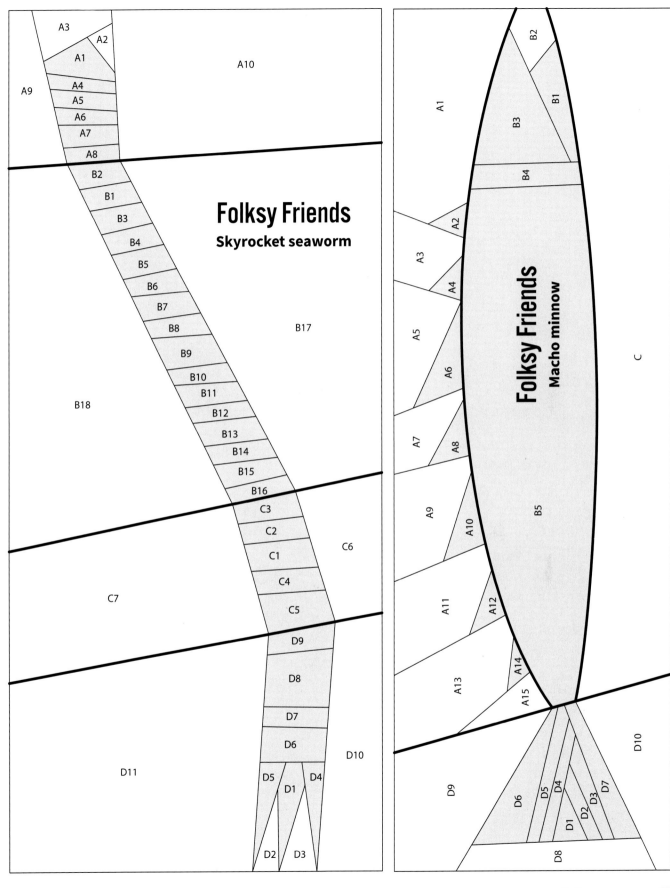

Folksy Friends
Skyrocket seaworm

Folksy Friends
Macho minnow

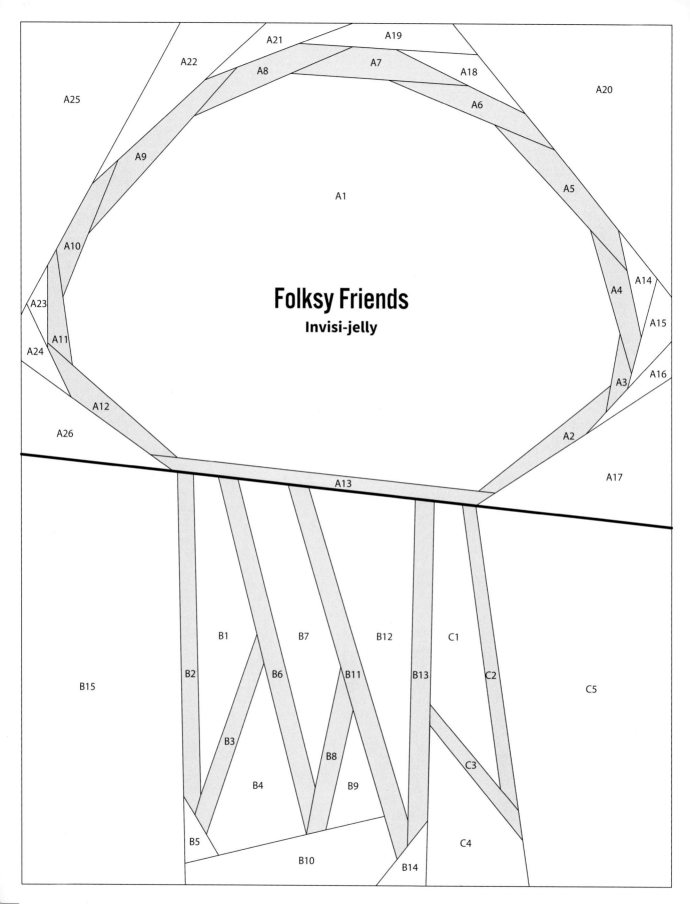

Folksy Friends
Invisi-jelly

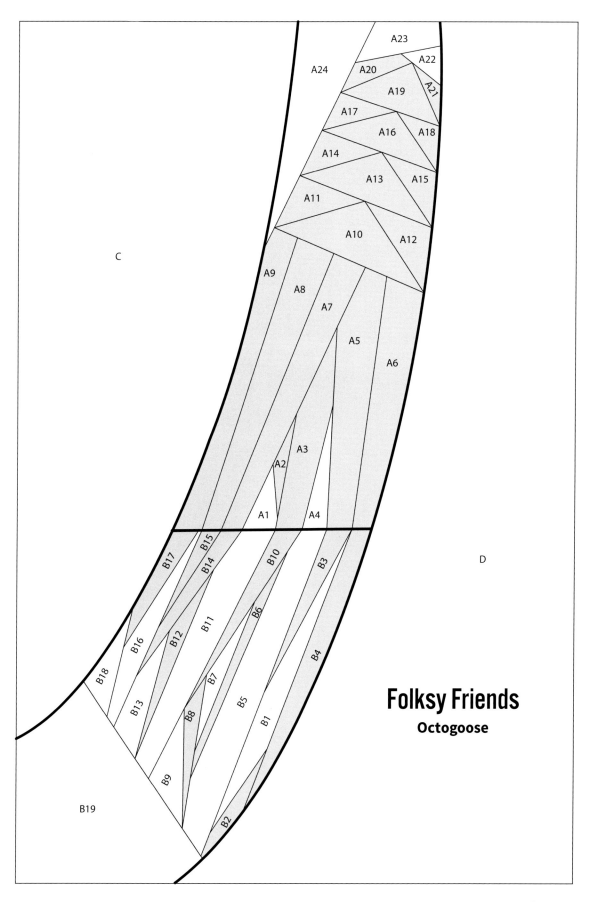

Folksy Friends
Octogoose

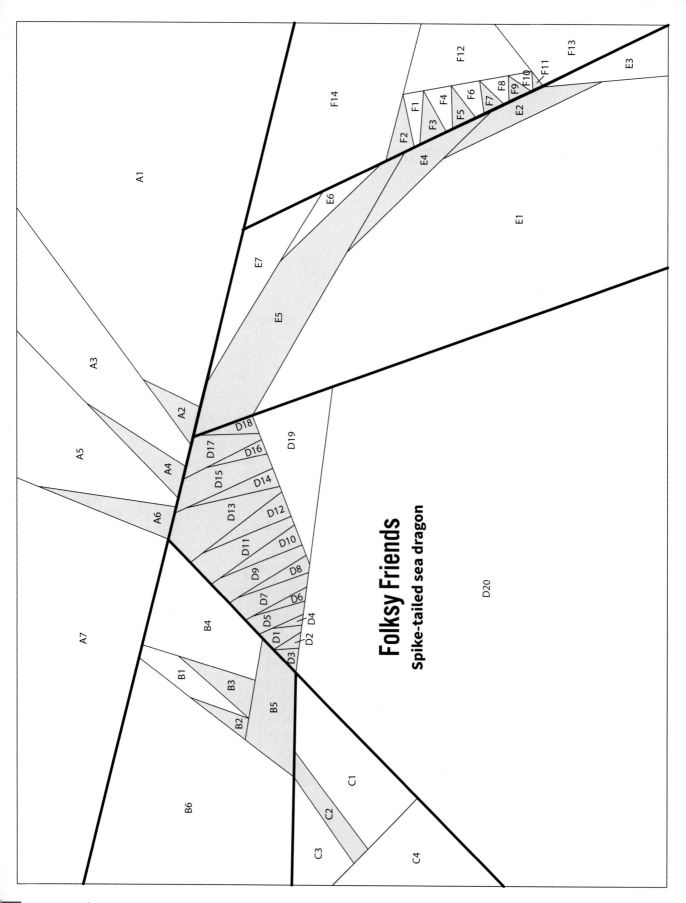

Folksy Friends
Spike-tailed sea dragon

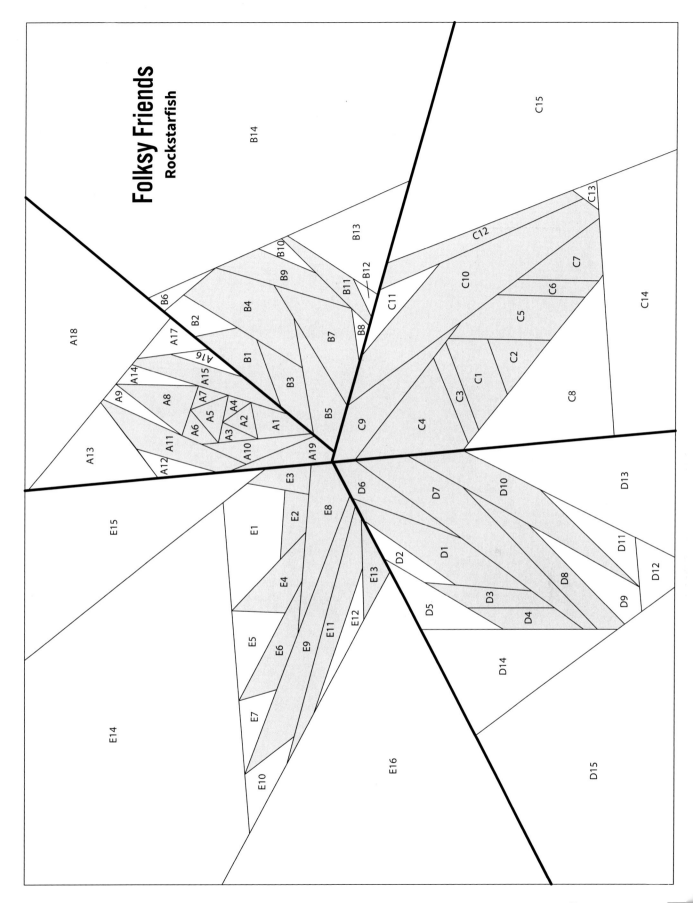

Folksy Friends
Rockstarfish

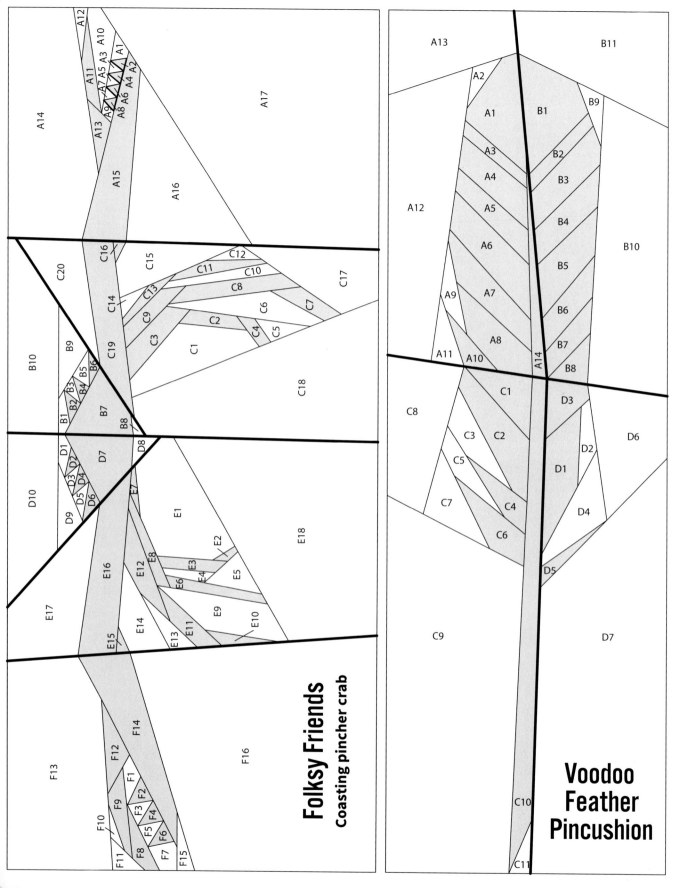

Folksy Friends
Coasting pincher crab

Voodoo Feather Pincushion

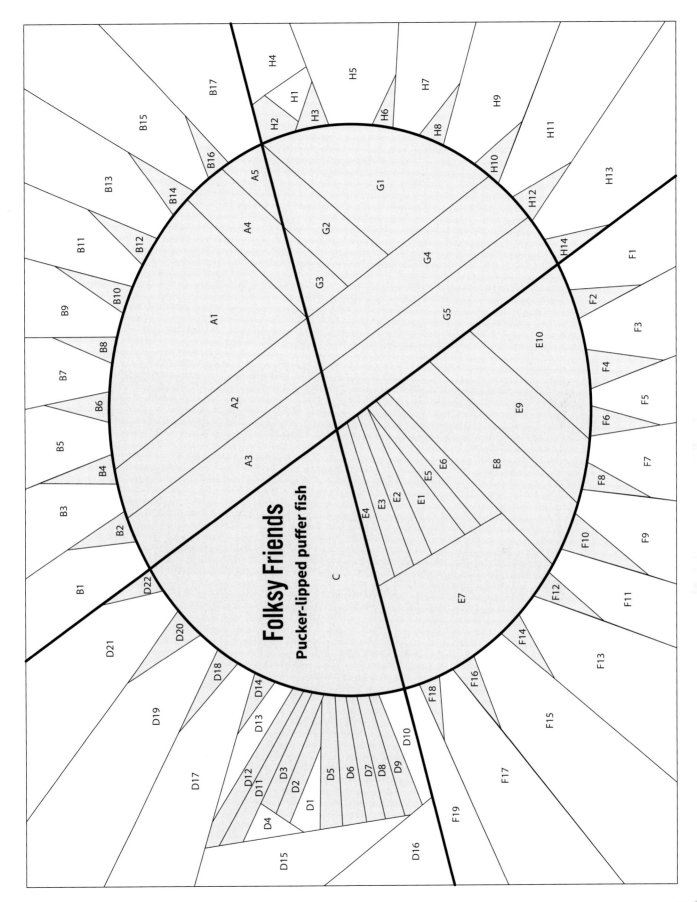

Folksy Friends
Pucker-lipped puffer fish

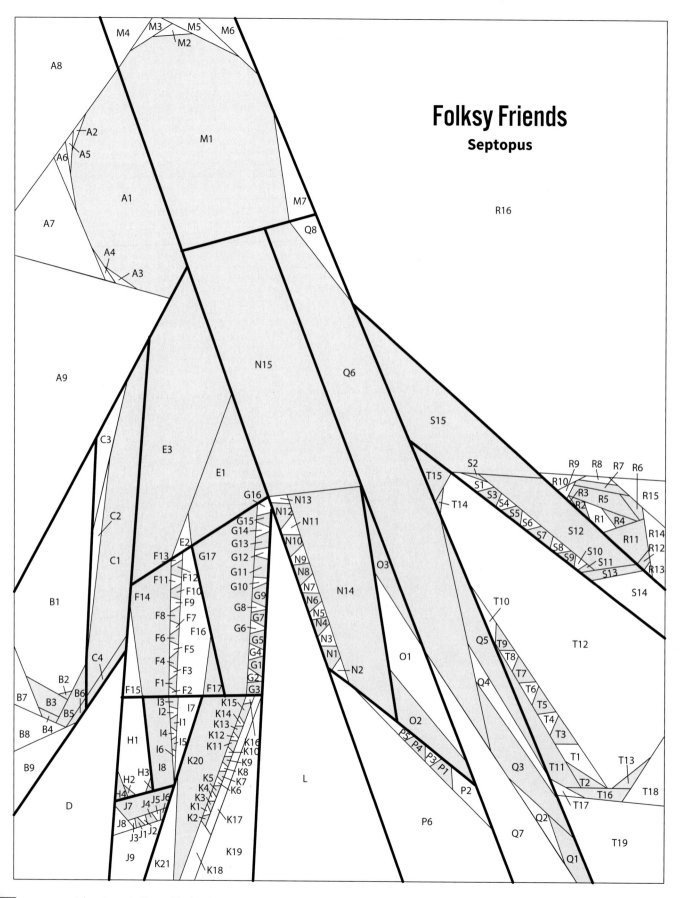

Folksy Friends
Septopus

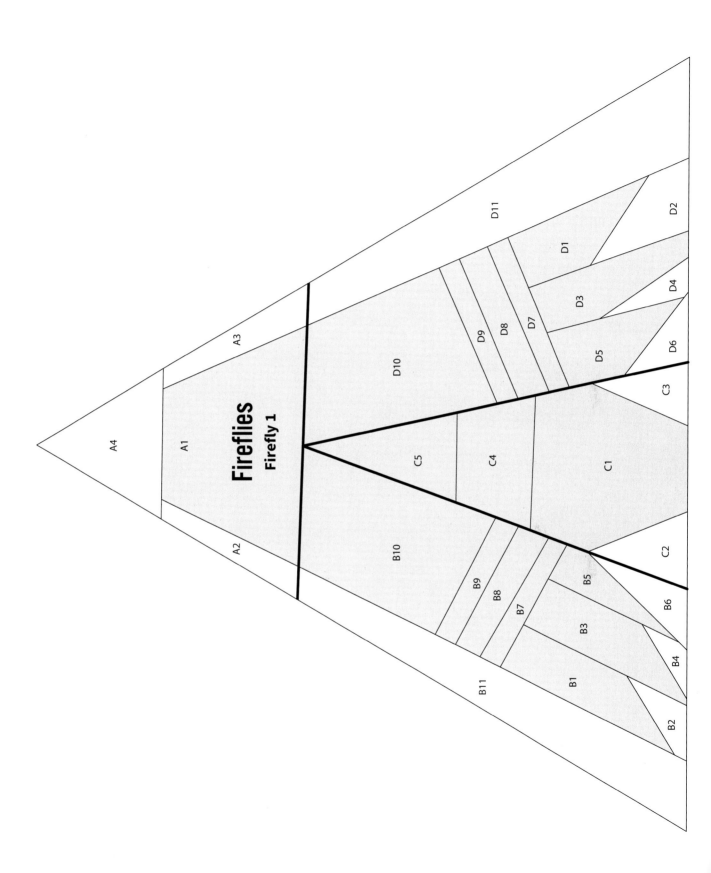

Fireflies
Firefly 1

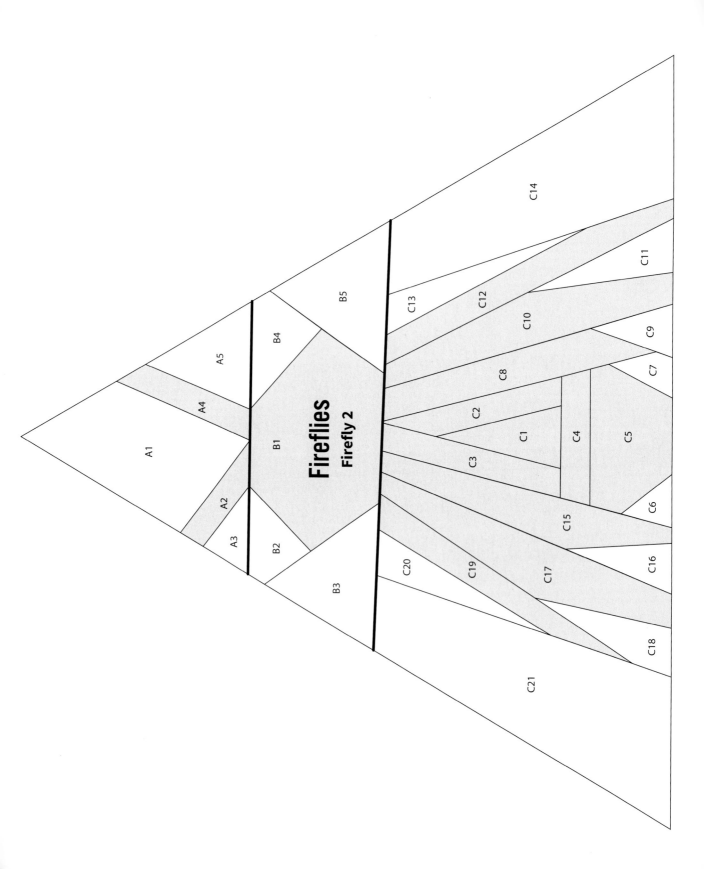

Fireflies
Firefly 2

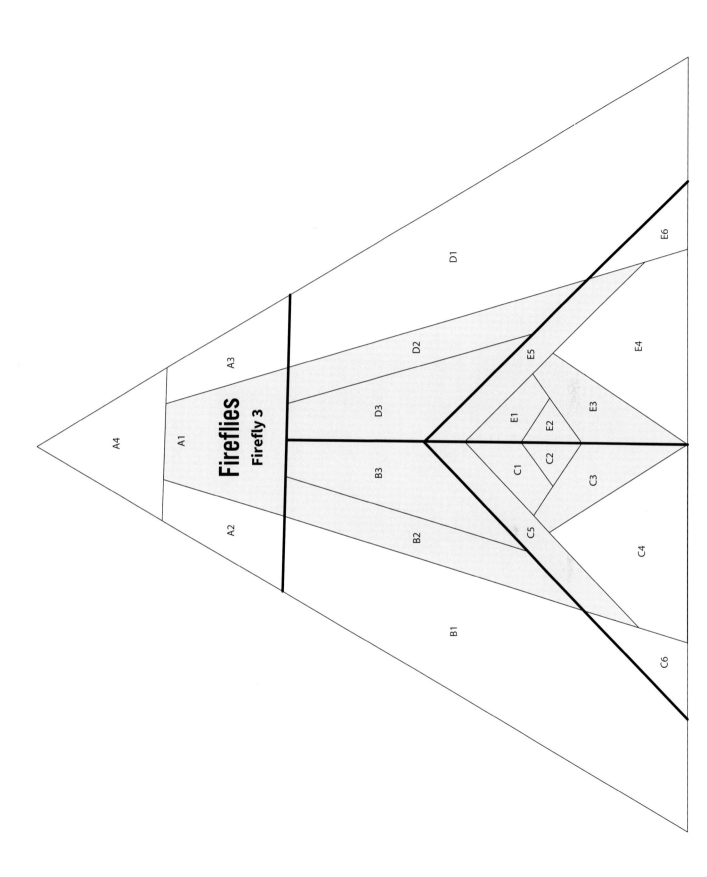

Fireflies
Firefly 3

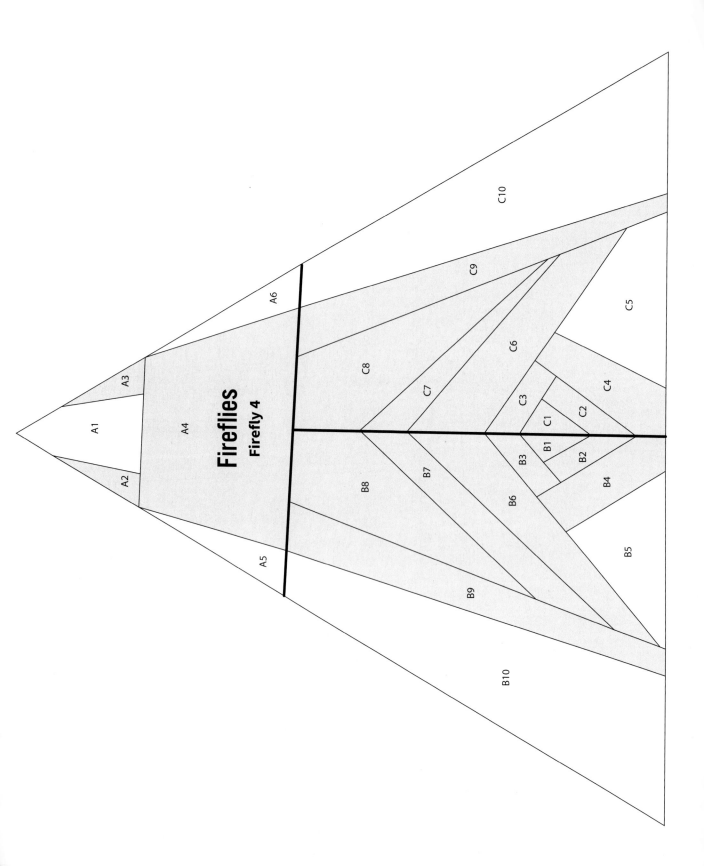

Fireflies
Firefly 4

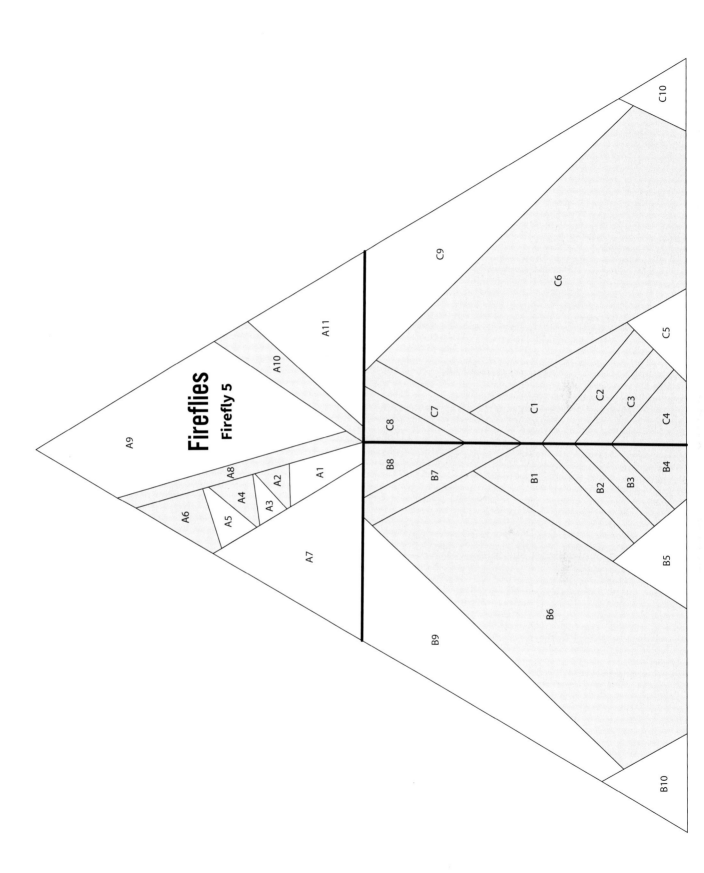

Fireflies
Firefly 5

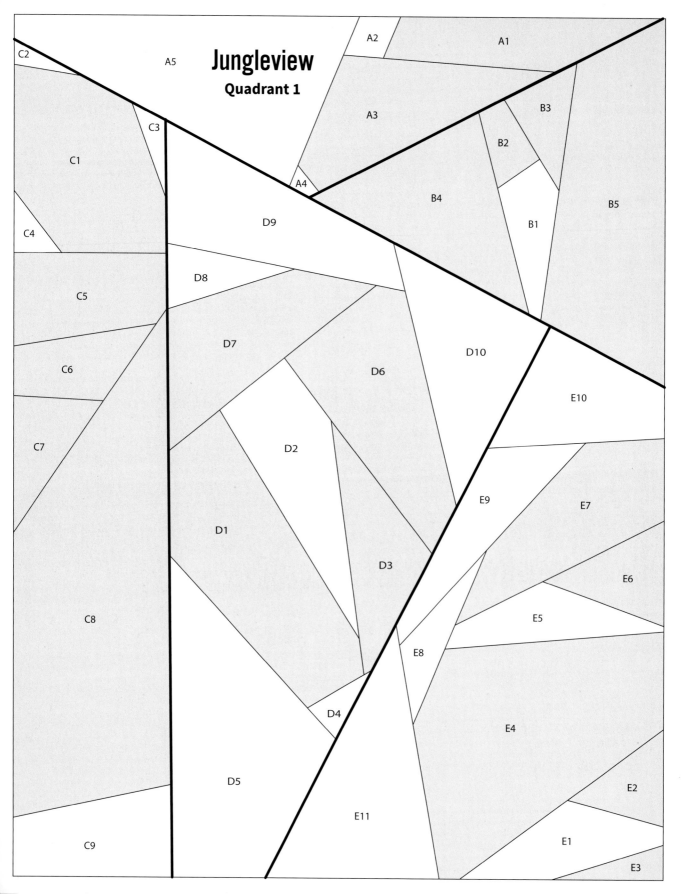

Jungleview
Quadrant 1

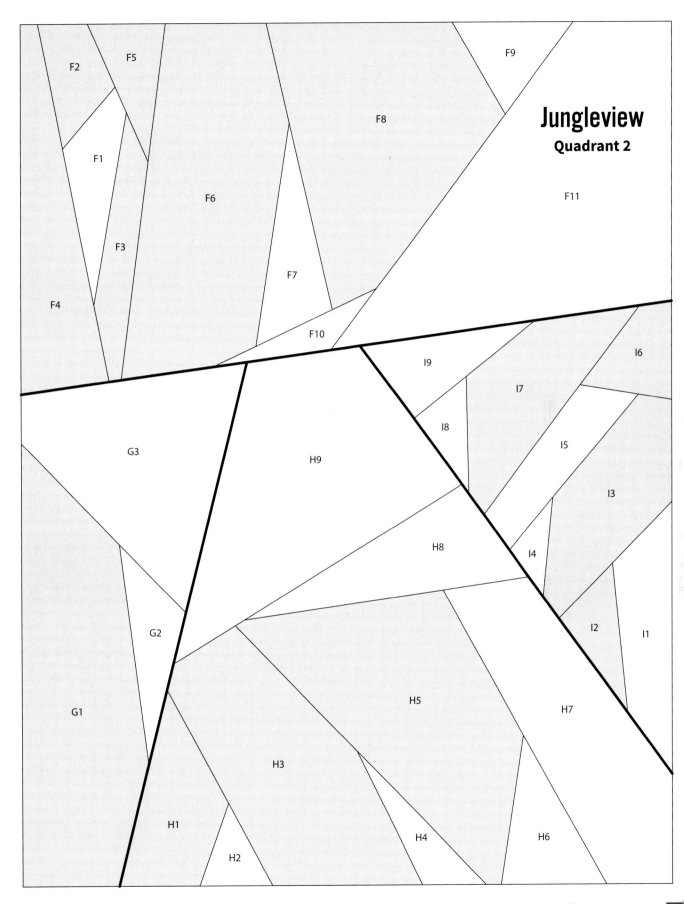

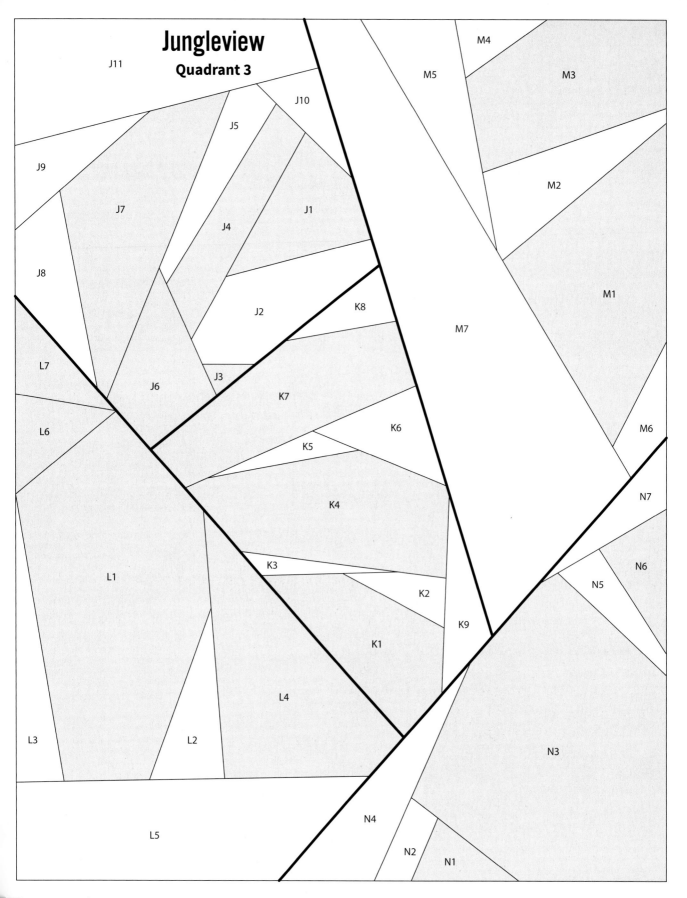

Jungleview
Quadrant 3

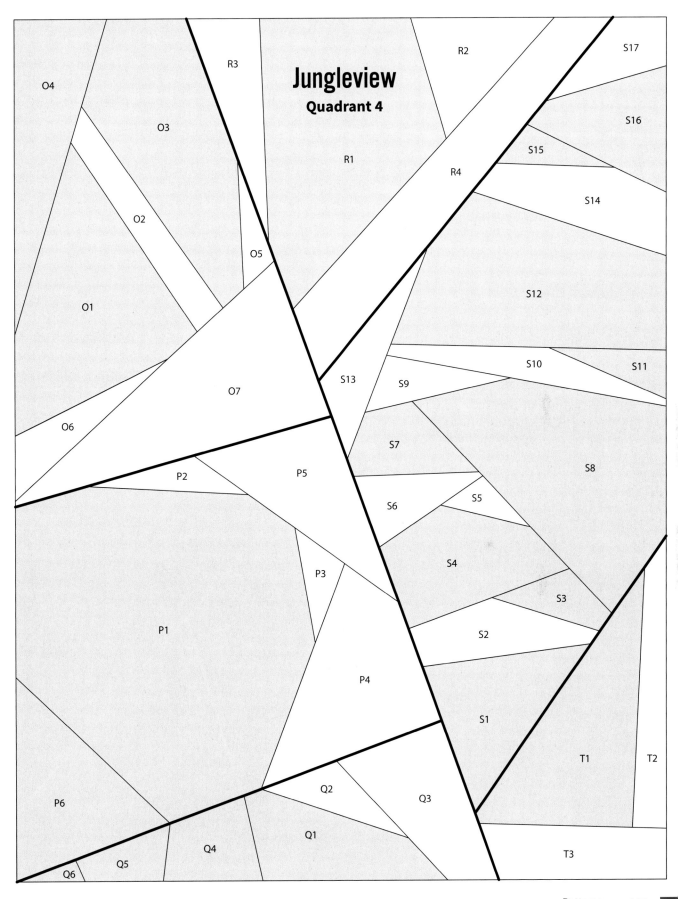

Jungleview
Quadrant 4

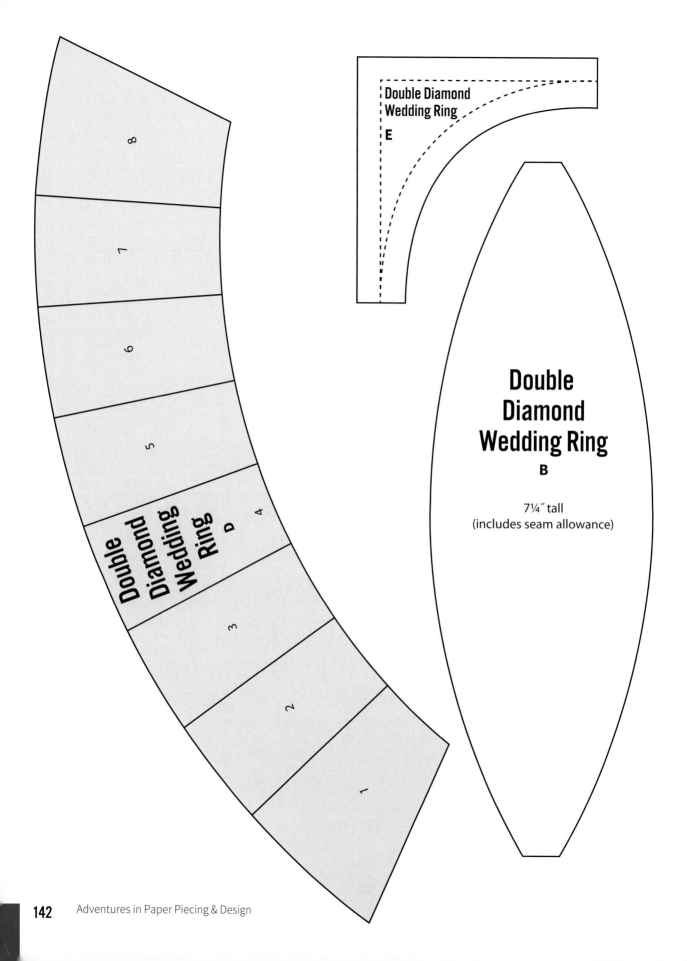

Double Diamond
Wedding Ring
E

Double
Diamond
Wedding Ring
B

7¼″ tall
(includes seam allowance)

Double
Diamond
Wedding
Ring
D

8

7

6

5

4

3

2

1

Double Diamond
Wedding Ring

A

Fold 10¼″ square into
quarters, then cut
along the solid lines
(includes seam allowance)

Center fold

Center fold

Double Diamond
Wedding Ring

C

2⅝″ square
(includes seam allowance)

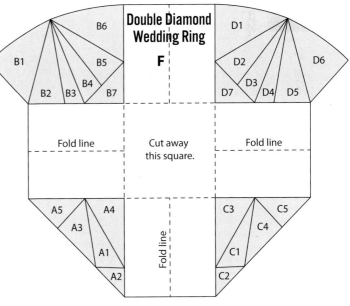

B6

B1

B5

B4

B2   B3   B7

Double Diamond
Wedding Ring

F

D1

D2

D3   D6

D4   D5

D7

Fold line

Cut away
this square.

Fold line

A5   A4

A3

A1

A2

Fold line

C3   C5

C4

C1

C2

About the Author

SARAH ELIZABETH SHARP has been making things for as long as she can remember. Her mother assumed she would grow up to be an artist; Sarah thought she would become an attorney (like her mother). Neither of them guessed she would do both, but that is exactly what she has set out to do.

Sarah's medium of choice is fabric. And while her quilting aesthetic might have traditional roots (think symmetry and grid structure), her method of thinking (and rethinking) through designs doesn't quite fit into any one category. She just makes whatever comes to mind and is thrilled by the prospect of sharing that passion with kindred spirits.

When Sarah is not busy creating or lawyering, she can be found at home in Indianapolis with her husband, three daughters, and misfit dog. Or traveling and seeing the world (minus the dog)—because she's always up for an adventure!

Follow Sarah on social media:

WEBSITE // nohatsinthehouse.com

INSTAGRAM // @nohatsquilts